CF7 Locom
From Cleburne to Everywhere

by Cary Franklin Poole

The Railroad Press

1150 Carlisle Street, Suite 444
Hanover, PA, 17331-1100

Printed in the United States of America by HBP, Hagerstown, Maryland.

International Standard Book Number 0-9657709-0-7

Dedication

This volume is dedicated to the men and women of the Santa Fe Cleburne Shops who labored to produce one of the most distinctive locomotive types built in the United States. They met the challenges the corporate office presented with creativity and ingenuity, and the final product was the CF7 locomotive. It was they who turned out the CF7 rebuild program. This is their story told through personal interviews, correspondence and conversations. While this story has been collaborated as best it could on the "corporate" side and through previously published accounts, it is meant to tell the "craft" side of a capital rebuild program conducted in the Cleburne Shops from 1970-1978. Though they met the challenge, I still feel few of the shop personnel could only imagine that so many of the products of their labor would still be toiling away on shortlines and in industrial settings around the U.S. and even in Mexico.

Locomotives often have labels attached to them, and the CF7 is certainly not without quite a few nicknames. But when beauty is viewed as being in the eye of the beholder, the railroad employees, both shop and train personnel, know the true beauty of the units in the fact the locomotives are safe, dependable and generally a step up from what they had been using previously.

Acknowledgements

I would like to acknowledge and thank the following people for their contributions to this publication:
First to Jaime F.M. Serensits, Publisher of The Railroad Press, for accepting this manuscript as his first book publication. I feel a sense of trust and respect was developed and nurtured solely through the benefit of the telephone, mail and e-mail systems. That trust led to this publication. I wish to thank Mr. Russell Tedder, President of Gloster & Southern and former President of Ashley, Drew & Northern Railroads, for providing the Introduction. When I first read it, I didn't want him to change a word; it tied all the chapters together with a single page of insight from a career railroader.

A special word of thanks needs to go to Eldon Whitworth, Program Coordinator for the Santa Fe CF7 rebuild project and Assistant General Foreman for the Back Shop, who answered numerous questions with a great deal of patience and expertise. Without him, the project simply would never have gotten off the ground. He answered my first call for information. The Cleburne Chronicle ran a public service announcement in a Sunday morning story on my search for information on the CF7 program. By coincidence, Mr. Whitworth's daughter read the story and telephoned her father when she remembered that he had been instrumental in the CF7 rebuild project. Mr. Whitworth's response has generated an enormous amount of information and contacts for this book.

I also wish to thank Jack Carlton, S. D. Rawlings, James Parker and W. F. Stepp for taking time to visit with me as well during the Cleburne Shop reunion.

I wish to thank the following individuals who have contributed photographs, slides and information to the project, and their contributions formed the nucleus for this manuscript. They are: Kel Aiken; Rich Anderson; Ken Ardinger; Peter Arnold; Jimmy W. Barlow; Rick Bartoskewitz; Gordon C. Bassett; Mike Bezilla; Joe Blackwell; C. C. Bobo; Ed Brooks, Manager of Industrial Development, Tennessee Southern Railroad Co.; H. E. Brouse; Dave Buccalo, WATCO; Perry Bush, CMO of the Columbus & Greenville Railway Co.; Wes Carr; Harold H. Carstens; Loren Casey; John Campbell, Kentucky Railroad Museum; Richard P. Campbell; Robert L. Carter; Jo Ann Condry, Amtrak Customer Satisfaction Advisor; Barry Crabtree, Tennken; Mike Curman, Yorkrail; Edward R. Dabler, Santa Fe Railway Historical & Modeling Society; Shane G. Deemer; Jeffrey Dobek; R.G. Edmonson; Emons Transportation; Joe H. Enochs; Walter R. Evans; Ted Ferkenhoff, S.E. Texas Chapter NRHS; Dick Finley, Indiana Rail Road; Bill Foster; Gregg Fuhriman; Ed Fulcomer; Dave Gallaspy, Econo-Rail; Paul Ganter; Bill Gillifillan; Brian Greibenow; Charles Haley, GM Inman Locomotive Services; Randy Hampton; Bill Harmon, Zuleka Productions; Kenneth Harrison; Michael Hasbargen, KCS Historical Society; Michael Herman; James E. Holder; Thomas Horvath; Steve Hottle; Todd Humphrey of Rainy Day Books; C.H. Humphreys; Stanley H. Jackowski; Bill Jasper, Rail Link; Brian L. Jennison; Allen R. Johnson; Gary Kazin; Allen Keller; Dan Keogh, Red River Valley & Western Railroad; Ben Kerr; Leo King; Stan Kistler, Santa Fe Railway Historical & Modeling Society; A. G. Coppinger; Robert A. LaMay; Bill Lang; Jay Leinbach; Bob Leverknight; Captain D. D. Lewis; Edward A. Lewis, Aberdeen & Rockfish Railroad Co.; Chris Long; Myrone Malone; Louis A. Marre; Ken Marsh; Michael A. Martin, Region Director, Media & Community Relations, BNSF; John B. McCall; R. F. McGowan, Amtrak V.P. Equipment and CMO; Joe McMillan; Scott Miller; Kenneth W. Moore; Laurie Morton, GE; Gary D. Munsey Sr.; Josh Musser; Steve Patterson; James F. Reed; Jay Reed, Rio Hondo Publishing; Vince Reh, Byron Hill Publishing; Matt Richie; Kent S. Roberts; Louis R. Saillard; Darrel Sawyer; Ed Shipper; Raymond C. Schmudde; Daniel M. Schroeder; Jim Shaw; Nancy Sherbert, Kansas State Historical Society; Joseph W. Shine, Four Ways West Publications; Tom Sink; Charles Slater; Steve Smedley; Fred W. Spurrell Jr.; Fred Strother, Plant Superintendent, Newton Asphalt Co. Inc. of Virginia; Jeff Sullivan, Mississippi & Skuna Valley Railroad; Thomas T. Taber; Al Trenholm, GM Eastern Illinois Railroad Co.; L. Gray Tuttle, Clinton Terminal Railroad Co.; WATCO; Evan L. Werkema; Roger Ziegenhorn; Mike Zollitsch; and all members of the Santa Fe Railway Historical & Modeling Society who helped. We also like to thank anyone we may have missed mentioning in the credits. A special thanks to Nolen Mears for proofreading and working with the rough drafts.

And lastly, I wish to thank my wife, Carole, who endures the long phone calls, conversations and field trips centering around railroading. She even insisted on riding with me to Rio Vista, Texas, to find C. W. Cramer's "stump" so she could have a better understanding of the full scope of the CF7 project. Thanks for your patience and understanding.

OPPOSITE: The Indiana Rail Road's scheme looks quite attractive on this CF7. The IRR started their operations with an all-CF7 roster; now they only have one left, #2543, as the rest have either been sold or scrapped. Photo by Bill Foster.

Table of Contents

ABOVE: Chattooga & Chickamauga's #103 poses outside of their facility at Lafayette, Georgia, on July 10, 1994. Unit previously owned by Columbus & Greenville, parent company of the C&C. Photo by Evan Werkema.

OPPOSITE: On June 26, 1986, freshly painted and newly arrived from the Cleburne shops, CF7's AD&N 1513 and GLSR 1501 are spotted in front of the Fordyce & Princeton depot (former Rock Island) at Fordyce, Arkansas, ready to back down into the F&P yard and pick up the daily southbound train for Crossett. Note the Santa Fe style numbers on the cab sides. Photo by Louis A. Marre.

Introduction

The CF7's are an important part of the story of the resurgence of shortlines in the last two decades. After their release on the second-hand locomotive market in the early 1980's, they became almost as common on shortlines as the ubiquitous General Electric 70-tonners were several decades ago.

My first acquaintance with CF7's came in the early 1970's while I was Vice President and General Manager of the Sabine River & Northern Railroad Company at Mulford (Orange), Texas. During this time I had frequent need to visit a new plant which SR&N's owners had built at Jasper, Texas, on the Santa Fe line. Santa Fe normally used two Geeps to boost braking for faster switching. It was fascinating to watch a pair of the shiny new CF7's briskly switching on the new plant lead, which was built around a curve on a high fill, and coming to a smooth stop before coupling to cars at the loading docks.

When word of the CF7 program got out, SR&N's shop foreman and I discussed buying one or two F-units and converting them to Geeps or roadswitchers in our shop to replace our two aging Alco 539's. For the same reason that Santa Fe's fleet of F's was available for conversion, similar units were on the market at prices well below GP7's or even RS2's or RS3's. For reasons now long forgotten, better judgment prevailed and the idea was never pursed, possibly because of the structural problems of the car body frames.

My first experience as a user of CF7's was after I became President of the Ashley, Drew & Northern Railway Company at Crossett, Arkansas. In November 1985, we needed motive power for a newly formed affiliate, the Gloster Southern Railroad, which operates 35 miles of former Illinois Central track between Gloster, Mississippi, and Slaughter, Louisiana. When we visited Cleburne, Texas, looking for a pair of locomotives for the new shortline, Luis Sanchez, Superintendent of Shops, pointed us to a long line of CF7's to pick from. We couldn't resist also picking out a pair to add to Ashley Drew & Northern's "Noah's Ark" fleet of paired GP28's, GP10's, SW1500's and SW1200's.

The ungraceful CF7's were equally at home as single units switching the large forest products manufacturing complex at Crossett or coupled for the 41-mile road turn to Monticello, Arkansas, with 60 to 75 car trains at up to 35 miles per hour over roller coaster grades. Their awkward appearance seemed to be somewhat alleviated when two units were coupled back to back or with another model. A CF7 and SW 1500 combination was an unusual, but impressive sight.

The AD&N's CF7's were also at home on its 57-mile sister company, the Fordyce & Princeton Railroad. Formerly a Rock Island branch, the F&P boasts grades and curves and ribbon rail which allow a pair of CF7's to hurry along with trains loaded with pulpwood, logs, cores and woodchips from the forests around Fordyce, Arkansas, to the mills at Crossett. Likewise, the two Gloster Southern units still run like clockwork down the former Illinois Central River Line. Since abandonment of the AD&N in 1996, its pair of CF7's are now part of the locomotive pool that works the Arkansas, Louisiana & Mississippi, another affiliated line between Crossett, Arkansas, and Monroe, Louisiana, and Fordyce & Princeton Railroads.

Experience in the years following our CF7 purchase proved it was one of the best locomotive decisions we ever made. With little repair and upkeep, they have proved to be more reliable than other units on the roster. Other owners report similar success.

Today the four CF7's dependably and predictably continue their daily chores. It appears that the ungainly workhorses will be plying shortline rails well into the 21st century. Like the proverbial battery powered rabbit, they just keep going and going.

Russell Tedder

The Need for New Power

When a railroad requires new motive power, the company usually has two options; the railroad could either purchase new motive power or convert existing power to new uses. The Illinois Central Railroad opted to rebuild Geeps in the mid-1960's, and other railroads began investigating the same possibility.

In the late 1960's, the Santa Fe faced the same set of options. As a result of this challenge, one of the more recognizable and distinguishable body shapes emerged in the form of the CF7 locomotive.

When the Santa Fe looked at new motive power from both Electro-Motive Division of General Motors and General Electric, it found the purchase price of a new locomotive to be at least $150,000, and in some cases, far exceeded this base price once options were added. The Santa

Fe had determined that a minimum of 200 units were needed to meet both marginal branch line and secondary main line use. With the purchase price for new units too high, the company chose the second option and began a search to determine if older power could be rehabilitated to meet new needs.

The search for adapting existing motive power soon focused on the 200-series F-units to determine if a complete overhaul was feasible and at what price per unit. The concept of the rebuild program was to produce a rebuilt unit for approximately $60,000, a third of what a new road-switcher locomotive would run. When the program was fully operating it was estimated the rebuilt units were running $40,000 per locomotive, far less than the original targeted price.

In looking at the 200-series F-units, the Santa Fe quickly discovered two problems. First, the units were in desperate need of overhaul and repair, as many of the units had run literally millions of miles across the Santa Fe system. Secondly, the carbody units were determined to be absolutely unsuitable for switching duty. The brakeman and engineer could not see the end of the train or where to spot cars without leaning out the cab window. Gordon Bassett, of the Cadillac & Lake City Railroad, said he "often cussed some poor railfan who moaned about the Santa Fe spoiling a beautiful F-unit." Since his railroad had no wye on the west end of a 60-mile stretch of track, he found the CF7 to have excellent front vision and rear vision -- as good as a hood unit could have. Mr. Bassett's line also rostered an ex-

ABOVE: Santa Fe F-unit #275L at Fort Worth, Texas, on May 5, 1975, three years before its conversion to a CF7. The unit would be the last F-unit converted, emerging as #2417. The unit now serves for Emons Transportation, painted in an Operation Lifesaver scheme for their subsidiary Yorkrail. Photo by James E. Holder, collection of Gordon C. Bassett.

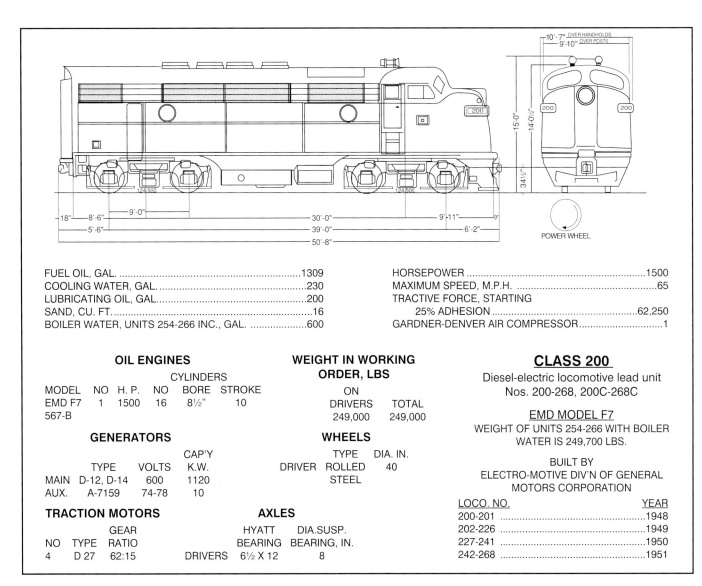

FUEL OIL, GAL.	1309
COOLING WATER, GAL.	230
LUBRICATING OIL, GAL.	200
SAND, CU. FT.	16
BOILER WATER, UNITS 254-266 INC., GAL.	600

HORSEPOWER	1500
MAXIMUM SPEED, M.P.H.	65
TRACTIVE FORCE, STARTING	
25% ADHESION	62,250
GARDNER-DENVER AIR COMPRESSOR	1

OIL ENGINES

MODEL	NO	H.P.	NO (CYLINDERS)	BORE	STROKE
EMD F7 567-B	1	1500	16	8½"	10

GENERATORS

	TYPE	VOLTS	CAP'Y K.W.
MAIN	D-12, D-14	600	1120
AUX.	A-7159	74-78	10

TRACTION MOTORS

NO	TYPE	GEAR RATIO
4	D 27	62:15

WEIGHT IN WORKING ORDER, LBS

ON DRIVERS	TOTAL
249,000	249,000

WHEELS

	TYPE	DIA. IN.
DRIVER	ROLLED STEEL	40

AXLES

	HYATT BEARING	DIA.SUSP. BEARING, IN.
DRIVERS	6½ X 12	8

CLASS 200

Diesel-electric locomotive lead unit
Nos. 200-268, 200C-268C

EMD MODEL F7
WEIGHT OF UNITS 254-266 WITH BOILER WATER IS 249,700 LBS.

BUILT BY
ELECTRO-MOTIVE DIV'N OF GENERAL MOTORS CORPORATION

LOCO. NO.	YEAR
200-201	1948
202-226	1949
227-241	1950
242-268	1951

Alaska F9 for a while and he had no desire to hang his head out a window to operate the unit in reverse in all sorts of weather over the course of 60 miles of track. His comments epitomized the full need to convert the F-units to road switchers.

The venerable F-units which had traveled so extensively over the Santa Fe system, first arrived in 1948. The units were delivered over five years from 1948 through 1953. With a couple of exceptions, the units were rated at 1500 horsepower and could deliver speeds of 65 miles per hour. The fuel capacity was 1309 gallons, with a lubricating oil capacity of 200 gallons. Cooling water capacity was 230 gallons. The traction gear ratio was 62:15 with 40-inch diameter wheels.

The F's started arriving in October 1948; eight units were delivered by year's end. This first batch of eight were delivered in the form of 200LABC and 201LABC. When delivery ceased five years later, the 200-series class was comprised of 326 F-units. The first eight were F3's and represented the only such units in the 200-series, with the remainder being F7's.

The Santa Fe determined the only way a complete overhaul could be accomplished was to remove the carbody and rebuild the unit into a conventional road-switcher, similar to the popular GP7/9 series that EMD produced in the late 40's and 50's.

Many a railfan commented under their breath that a magnificent F-unit was going to be cut-up to create something so utilitarian and ugly as the CF7. But the CF7 was to fill a much needed niche, an inexpensive versatile road unit which could be employed as a switcher if needed be. Once the Santa Fe had decided on the rebuild program, it initially offered the project to both EMD and GE. Both companies refused on the grounds their engineers did not feel the conversion could take place. After all, the engineers felt that once the car body was cut through and removed, the structural integrity of the locomotive would be lost and the unit would suffer constantly from a sagging frame.

C. W. Cramer was the Superintendent of the Cleburne Shop when the Santa Fe

went looking for a facility to handle the rebuilding program. W. E. Jack Carlton, a former trainmen and now a noted local historian and author, retold how the request was conveyed from Chicago to Cleburne. The caller asked if a geep could be rebuilt from a 200-class F-unit. Mr. Charles W. Cramer had a knack, as one would say, of "always being noted for his polite manner and ability to turn a cultured phrase." His supposed response was later translated into, "Why yes, certainly; my fine boys can do that!" Someone who actually was told the real response said that it was a simple, "Hell yes, send it down!" referring to the F7 #262C. He was determined to take the remains of a five-million mile veteran, and turn it into a new locomotive type, the CF7.

Counting on Mr. Cramer's determination and the general high experience level of the Cleburne Shop personnel, Santa Fe proceeded with an initial order to rebuild six units. After assessing these prototypes, a determination would later be made as to whether or not additional F-units would be converted into CF7's.

Cleburne History

The placement of a major rebuilding facility in Cleburne, Texas, was a reward to the community for services rendered during one of the numerous yellow fever outbreaks which often struck the Texas coast areas. Cleburne serves as the county seat of Johnson County and was founded as a community around 1854. The community was first known as Camp Henderson, but Confederate soldiers returning from the war renamed the town after Major General Pat Cleburne, an Irish-born general known for his extreme tenacity and fearlessness in battle. General Cleburne and fellow Texan, Brigadier General H. B. Granbury, were two of five generals lost by the Confederacy during the Battle of Franklin. Returning veterans from Texas named the community after General Cleburne, and the nearby community of Granbury was named after the other fallen general.

The Santa Fe predecessor, the Gulf, Colorado and Santa Fe, was informed on October 16, 1898, that Galveston (general headquarters for the railroad), was to be placed under a yellow fever quarantine. Fearing the railroad operations would be suspended over the entire line, a special passenger train was ordered to carry railroad men and families north to escape the quarantine.

The General Manager, Colonel L. J. Polk, directed the train northward at 9:00 p.m. and it traveled approximately an hour until it entered the community of Alvin, Texas. The local residents were not willing to allow the train to stop because of the mislead belief that the passengers were carrying yellow fever. A shotgun-toting crowd allowed the engine to take on water, but only outside the city limits.

The train continued northward to Brenham and later Temple, meeting the same fate at both locations where the locals would not allow the passengers off due to fear of contaminating the towns-people with yellow fever. The train had been dubbed the "Yellow Fever Special" and telegraph messages were being sent up and down the line to warn other communities of the train's approach. But, when the train rolled into Cleburne, much to all the passengers surprise, the local townspeople welcomed the refugees into their community. A band even turned out to play and rooms were offered in private homes for the passengers.

Following the great Galveston Hurricane of 1900 and after a couple more yellow fever outbreaks, the Santa Fe was ready to relocate portions of its operations over the entire system and de-centralize the importance of Galveston. The limited facilities, under the directorship of John Player, had been requested to convert switchers from the 0-8-0 type into 2-8-0 locomotives. Mr. Player established Cleburne very early on with the Santa Fe as a community with a "can-do" attitude. After reviewing the excellent job the Cleburne shops did on the 2-8-0 steam rebuild program, Cleburne became the major rebuild facility for the entire system.

Two other factors had also played important roles in why Cleburne became a major rebuild facility. In the late 1800's, the Santa Fe had started to convert its locomotives from coal to oil burning fuel. With the Cleburne facility, the Santa Fe found itself directly-in and adjacent-to two of the largest oil producing states in the nation in the form of Texas and Oklahoma.

The second factor was a direct result of action taken by the citizens of Cleburne. When the residents realized Santa Fe was looking for a shop site, the residents purchased a 106 acre lot in order to sweeten the deal. The lot was offered as an incentive to locate the facility in Cleburne.

Partly due to luck, chance and their own initiatives, the citizens of Cleburne insured prosperity for the entire communi-ty for nearly a century in the form of a locomotive shop, car shop and coach repair facility. By simple hospitality and initiative, Cleburne added immensely to its tax base. The Santa Fe alone was con-tributing $125,000 per month in 1905 for wages and the amount only continued to swell, as the monthly payroll hit $460,000 in 1950.

In the 1920's, approximately 1200 men were employed in the shops. Of this number, about one-half were mechanics; the balance consisted of laborers, helpers and apprentices. A well-organized student program was centered in the Cleburne Shops where inexperienced youths were apprenticed in a series of instruction and hands-on-skills. Apprentices in the freight car department were instructed over a period of three years and apprentices in the passenger and locomotive departments for four years.

Not only did the apprentices receive instruction involving actual working condi-tions, but in addition, for two nights a week in two-hour sessions, they were instructed in mechanical drawing, mathe-matics, and other technical skills.

The apprenticeship supplied not only a skilled labor pool for the railroad, but also served to instill a powerful sense of loyalty to the railroad. The apprentices learned not only the "how-to" of perform-ing a skill, but also the "why" that was involved in the task as well.

Young men who did not have family in the immediate area were housed at the YMCA. The YMCA charged a $1.00 for the apprentice to stay. The facility was located next to the railroad between Willingham and Wardville Streets. Many families had to sign for their child to enter the apprentice program, whereafter he had to obey the rules of the railroad. Those rules included not being able to cuss or use tobacco products, and live in a regimented environment.

OPPOSITE: The first CF7, ATSF #2649, ex-262C, is seen in Emporia, Kansas, in March of 1979, after repainting into Santa Fe's warbonnet scheme. Much has changed since the unit rolled out of the Cleburne Shops nine years ago, in February of 1970 (page 45); the frame has been closed, the old crank-style windows were replaced and an orange warning beacon was added. The step edges are now yellow and the trucks are silver. Photo by Roger Ziegenhorn, collection of Gordon C. Bassett.

The Rebuild Program

The decision of the Santa Fe to begin such a remarkable and extensive rebuild program centered on two men -- Larry Cena, Vice President of Santa Fe Operations and Henry N. Chastain, General Manager and Chief Mechanical Officer. In 1969, it was Mr. Cena who asked Mr. Chastain if an F-unit nose could be cut off to create a road switcher. Chastain reportedly responded, "No, because of the way EMD built them in the first place." He was referring to the frame work built into the car bodies. But he quickly countered his first comment with, "but they can be built into Geeps." After hastily drafting sketches of what Chastain thought the new Geep should look like, the information was passed on to Santa Fe President, John S. Reed. Based on preliminary plans and estimates for rebuilding an F-unit into a Geep, Reed asked that Cena appoint the project to the Cleburne Shops.

In making their decision, the Santa Fe also hoped to reap tax advantages as they related to rebuilt locomotives. In the 1970's, the tax laws stated a substantially rebuilt locomotive could be depreciated over several years as if the locomotive were new. Coupled with this new depreciation cycle, the railroad could also receive an investment tax credit. The process of depreciating the cost of a new locomotive and receiving an investment tax credit was generally referred to as a Capital Rebuild Program. One of the few restrictions on the depreciation is that the rebuild costs had to exceed half of the original purchase price. The locomotive could then be depreciated over the usual period of eight to fifteen years. With both a tax benefit and a large highly-skilled shop in Cleburne, Texas, Chastain, Cena and Reed felt the project could succeed. They did, however, have very valid concerns about what stock holders and other corporate officers would think if the program did fail. After all, both EMD and GE had turned down the project and the railroad management certainly did not want an embarrassment on its hands. It was this concern regarding failure and embarrassment, that caused a good portion of the project to be launched secretly.

Once the decision was made to proceed with the conversion project, Lee Townsley, from the Topeka, Kansas, shops, came down and instructed the welders where to make the precise cuts on the #262C. The idea was to cut just to the rear of the windshield to the front coupler and just behind the electrical cabinet to the rear coupler. Once these two cuts had been completed, the long and short hoods of the carbody came off intact and were removed by a crane to be deposited in a scrap gondola. Mac Vickers and Eldon Whitworth were the two men who worked to remove the carbody as instructed by Lee Townsley.

Work began on the #262C in fall of 1969. D. C. McCandless and Eldon Whitworth, both of whom volunteered for the program, worked overtime on separate shifts to complete the project. What emerged from the Shop a few months

BELOW: An eclectic lashup consisting of early CF7 2630 with F-unit 236C and a rare GP7B cabless unit 2792A is seen at Brownwood, Texas. Collection of Allen R. Johnson.

later, was the #2649, the first CF7. Two hundred thirty-two other units would follow over the next eight years.

Early word of the rebuild program labeled the new locomotive as a GP8, similar to the units the Illinois Central was turning out at their Paducah, Kentucky, facility. After its release in February 1970, almost a full year passed before the official designation of CF7 was publicized and confirmed by the Santa Fe Railroad.

The #2649 was a unique locomotive, not only because it was the first CF7, but because it was used as an experiment to establish the pattern for other units to follow. This particular unit featured the only set of dynamic brakes to be found on a CF7. This was due the fact a long hood from a wrecked GP7B (#2788A) with dynamic brakes was on hand and the CF7 was constructed from this available hood. Later units utilized a long hood, minus dynamic brakes, which was fabricated in the Cleburne Shops. In order to get the GP7 hood on the frame of the former F-unit, 7 inches had to be cut from the bottom of the hood where the hood connected to the main frame and running board.

The #2649 also had smaller steps than the following units. It was determined by feedback from trainmen that in later

units there was a need to enlarge the steps to allow brakemen better footing. In praising the qualities of the locomotive, many crewmen remembered the large and lowered steps. They felt this added greatly to the safety of switching operations. Gordon Bassett reported that the "railings and grab irons were well placed; there was a handle where you needed it." He further commented that the steps were "slanted out so they were easy to climb on and you could stand comfortably on the bottom step while switching." On a negative side, Charles Slater of the Los Angeles Junction Railroad commented on the steps of the #2554. After a very short stay on the LAJ, it was determined the unit could not take sharp curves because the steps jutted out too far and shortly after entering service, struck a concrete slab. The steps, needless to say, were torn off of the locomotive and the unit was quickly replaced.

When the CF7 is compared to locomotives which were pressed into switching duties, it compares favorably. The steps on a U23B were said to be "nearly vertical and resembled climbing a book case." GP9's were not considered much better, but the men who had to switch using an F-unit, said the carbody was "hell for switching."

The #2649 was the longest in rebuild, with the job taking from October 1969 until February 1970. Because of various dignitaries who kept visiting, it would often be rolled out with the electrical connections incomplete. It would generally take the crew a couple of days to prep the unit for inspection and another couple of days to get it back to where it could be further modified after each visit. During these inspection visits, the unit often had open holes in the steel deck and plywood covering the holes.

Eldon Whitworth, Program Coordinator for the CF7, often commented he "was sure happy after each visit that someone had not tried themselves or insisted on having the starter button tested." Nothing would have happened because the electrical connections were incomplete or not connected during the inspections.

One of the modifications made on the #2649 and not on subsequent units was the adding of deck plate steel. With the carbody removed, it was determined the side sills needed additional shoring up and the ½-inch deck plate was replaced with 1½-inch deck plate. It was then determined that the extra plate was excessive and not added to other units. After the

#2649, it was decided the side sills would be sufficient in preventing the frame from sagging.

The paint job on the unit was completed long before all of the electrical connections and electrical cabinet work was installed, partly due to the many inspections the unit was subjected to. The unit left the shop in the Santa Fe navy blue with yellow trim paint scheme. The #2649 also had several thousands of miles on it from various test runs and inspections before being assigned to mainline service.

The official unveiling took place in Dallas, Texas, on Friday, March 13, 1970. The media and the public were welcome to greet the #2649 as it made its first official public appearance. In actuality, the unit had been on the road for a few weeks while tests were being conducted.

It has often been speculated by railfans that the #2649 was used as a yard goat for the Cleburne Shops. Contrary to this belief, the unit served on the open road for Santa Fe and was at one time assigned as a local switcher at Clovis, New Mexico. Ironically, the #2649 met its own fate as a scrapped unit, with parts contributing to rebuild two F3 units for the Anthracite Historical Railway Society. Since the #2649 had the additional 1½-inch of steel deck, Mr. Whitworth said that he pitied the man who had to cut up that particular unit.

The men and women of the Cleburne Shops were trying to achieve two goals when the CF7 program began. First, the converted units were to save money over the purchase price of a new locomotive. Secondly, ease of maintenance was an important factor. Many would claim the CF7 to be the ugliest, or at best, the plainest of locomotives to be produced. However, its basic utilitarian features are evident when you look at the ease of maintaining the unit.

A unique feature which emerged early in the program was a new style of cut lever. The lever was designed for a brakeman to make the cut while standing on the steps or front walkway of the locomotive. This contrasts from the standard practice of having the brakeman always on the ground to make a cut. The Santa Fe chose not to patent this design, but was ever-vigilant on keeping EMD and GE personnel out of sight of the new lever. Neither GE or EMD employees were allowed to photograph the cut lever nor were their personnel left alone long enough to sketch the lever. Only when the first CF7's started hitting the road in the early 1970's did GE and EMD start including the same cut lever design on their locomotives.

Joe Blackwell, an engineer who used the CF7 in the early 1980's, spoke very

highly of the newly designed cut lever and said that type of cut lever was especially useful before crew members began to carrying packset radios.

Once the project began in earnest, a production schedule was established. Two-hundred thirty three units were rebuilt from February 1970 until March 1978, which approximated Santa Fe's need of a minimum of 200 units for branch line work and switching. The numbering system utilized by the Santa Fe started with the #2649 and went in descending order to #2417. The program concluded when there were simply no more F-units on the Santa Fe roster to convert. Twenty-four F-units were not converted due to wrecks and it was determined the rebuild on these units was not feasible. In addition to F7's, F3's and F9's were converted as well.

Even the name "CF7" had some contradictions to it. Officially, Santa Fe referred to the program as the "converted F7", hence the name CF7. However, the men and women of the Cleburne Shops were just as firmly convinced that the "C" stood for Cleburne, Texas, where the rebuild took place. In one other rebuild situation, the Santa Fe used the initials "SSB" to represent the Switcher-San Bernardino rebuild project, which was hosted by the San Bernardino, California, facility.

With the completion of the 2649, production began in earnest. Peak production was reached in 1977; after that point, the production trailed off on the CF7's, but escalated with the GP7 rebuild program. As the Cleburne Shop moved through the eight year production of CF7's, subtle changes emerged in the units, particularly in certain batches that were completed at the same time. This production schedule explains some of the confusion over round versus angled cabs and two versus four stack exhaust systems and other minor changes. The program was, simply put, ever-changing as feedback was provided by trainmen and when additional cost-cutting techniques could be employed.

Primary construction of the CF7 took place in the Cleburne Boiler and Coach Shops from 1970 until 1976, when the Coach Shop burned. For the last two years of the program, the Boiler Shop remained the principal rebuild facility and was quite cramped until the end of the program.

The rebuild of an F7 to a CF7 generally took 45 days from the time an F-unit entered the shop to have the fuel tanks pumped out and steamed to the final inspection and assignment back into the system. After the rebuild was completed, each unit spent eight to sixteen hours undergoing electrical load tests. After the load tests were completed, each unit was

tested in the field with a run from Cleburne to Dallas and back. A punch-list was developed for each unit and each craft (union trade) was then allowed to complete any necessary adjustments or repairs.

The shop had schedules of three, four and five days. The average schedule was to release a unit every four days, but certain cycles mandated a unit to be released every five or sometimes even every three days.

It should be noted that the Cleburne Shop and suppliers such as GE and EMD often did not see eye to eye on production priorities. The replacement parts were often hard to come by because the suppliers often did not honor promises made to keep production schedules on time.

In order to meet the "1201 report," a reported forwarded to the corporate office in Chicago listing the production schedule, personnel often had to raid newly arriving units of sorely needed parts. As locomotives arrived with bad orders, the Cleburne men pulled these parts off the units to put on CF7's in an effort to keep the production schedule intact.

Once the program was fully underway, many of the shop men remembered, the F-units would come in during the afternoon and evening and would be deposited on track #18. By the next day the stripping process began in earnest when the locomotive was de-wheeled using an overhead crane and would be set immediately on Track #9 to complete further stripping.

The assembly line for CF7's did not even remotely resemble Henry Ford's straight line process. Rather, the assembly and rebuilding was conducted on parallel tracks within the Boiler Shop. This allowed each craft to work on the units in sequence and not concurrently. All but tracks 1 through 7 of the Boiler Shop were dedicated to the CF7 rebuild program.

The CF7 program was considered to be a complete rebuild, from the trucks to the cab. In doing so, everything was removed from the frame and rebuilt back on the locomotive.

The prime mover was of a vital concern to the Santa Fe Railroad. Number-wise, the F7 was second only to the GP9 in the number built utilizing the 567B prime mover, with a total production of 3849 units. The prime mover involved, the EMD 16-567B, was a sixteen cylinder engine. This was the same prime mover used in the F2A and B units, the F3A and B units and the F7B locomotives. Most CF7's got the 567BC engine; the first two CF7's, #2649 and #2648, were the only exceptions, employing the 567B engine. The 567BC was an upgrade which utilized a B head coupled to C liner. Water jumpers cooled the C liners. This resulted

OCT. 4, 1971
MAR. 15, 1977
APR. 1, 1980

FORMERLY L & C F7
Identified until April 1, 1980 as 2500 CLASS

<u>**CLASS 2417**</u>
LOCO NOS. 2417-2649
CF7

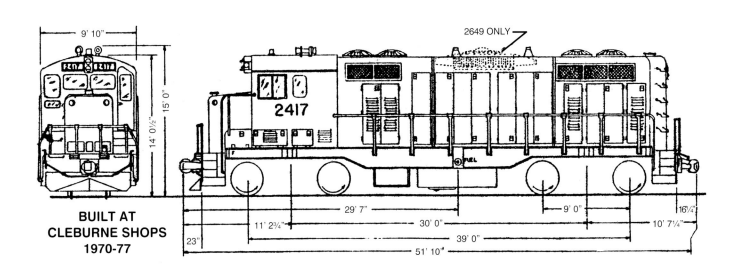

2649 ONLY

9' 10"

15' 0"

14' 0½"

BUILT AT
CLEBURNE SHOPS
1970-77

2417

29' 7"

9' 0"

16¼"

11' 2¾"

30' 0"

10' 7¼"

23"

39' 0"

51' 10"

TOTAL UNITS 228   (CF7 2417-2649)   CLASS   2417

Composite photo of Yorkrail's Operation Lifesaver unit 1500. This was the last CF7 built by Santa Fe (former #2417). Picture was produced by combining several photos taken of different sections of the unit. View shows great detail of the placement of the louvers and the side cab windows. It also shows off the step edges, the grabirons and the railings. This is the last CF7 built and keeps many of its as-built features such the extra side cab window (some railroads had plated these over) and the extra engineer's window in the front. Many CF7's received one large window on the front to replace the smaller two windows. The yellow paint also shows the side door panels off very well. Photos by Jaime F.M. Serensits.

First Issued - Apr. 1, 1980
Revised - Jan. 1981, Dec. 1983

UNITS FROM 2417
TO INCLUSIVE 2649

CLASS   2417

Horsepower 1500	Journal Bearings ....Hyatt
Diesel Engine Type ....Ⓐ..567 BC	Journal Size - Inches ....6½ x 12
R.P.M..800	Motor Support Journal Size - In. 8
Main Generator D12	Wheel Diameter - Inches 40
Traction Motors D27	Weight Front Truck - Lbs 124,690
Air Conditioning ....VAPOR	Weight Rear Truck - Lbs. 124,310
Air Compressor ....GD-WXO	Total Loco. Weight - Lbs. 249,000
Air Brake Schedule ....Ⓑ.....26L	Weight on Drivers - Lbs. 249,000
Multiple Unit Connections.......................F&R	Gear Ratio...62:15
Sand Capacity - Cu. Ft. 19	Cont. Tractive Eff. - Lbs. 41,300
Fuel Capacity - Gallons ....Ⓒ.1255	Min. Cont. Speed - M.P.H. 11.0
Lube Oil Cap. - Gallons 200	Max. Track Curvature ....23 deg.
Cooling Water Cap. - Gal. 240	

Ⓐ Units 2648 & 2649 ....567B Engine
Ⓑ Upgraded units after 12-1-78. Began with 2677. All others have 24-RL equipment.
Ⓒ 2643, 2644, 2645 & 2649 ....1330 Gal.

The diagram, measurements and specs are from Santa Fe's locomotive "notebook". Format changed for clarity and readability.

in a relatively inexpensive upgrade.

The decision to stay with the 567 engine was a wise one, as the engine had a long and dependable history. The 567 was developed in 1937 and continued in production until 1966. The numbers refer to the bore stroke of 8½-inch bore with a 10-inch stroke for a displacement of 567 cubic inches. Early in the design stage, EMD hoped to produce engines in three sizes, a 6-cylinder 600 horsepower model, a 12-cylinder 1000 horsepower model and a 16-cylinder 1350 horsepower model. The idea was to create a versatile engine developing different horsepower ratings, but employing interchangeable cylinders and pistons.

It is speculated that the development of the 567 engine allowed EMD to gain mastery of the diesel locomotive market over the other locomotive builders, even though the other companies did build a limited line of diesel-electrics. The War Production Board had mandated other builders (Alco, Baldwin, Lima, etc.) to continue production of steam locomotives and allowed EMD to concentrate on diesels. This contention is based on three facts. First, EMD toured #103, a set of FT's in A-B-B-A fashion across the country in which the locomotive set racked up 83,764 miles in 1939. This was the first major test for the 567 prime mover and it helped familiarize 20 different railroads with the capabilities of the diesel freight engine. The reliability of the prime mover convinced many railroad corporate officers of the merits of long haul diesel locomotives.

The Santa Fe also helped prove the reliability of the 567 engine when it applied to the Office of Defense Transportation for help in eliminating war-caused freight jams. By mid-1943, the tempo of the war had turned and the need to haul military-related cargo escalated to unforeseen proportions. Since the Santa Fe crossed vast expanses of arid and mountainous terrain, water was at a premium, and steam locomotives needed water.

With millions of gallons of water needed, the problem was only aggravated when helpers were needed on the mountain lines. As more freight was hauled, more water was needed. The water had to be trucked or transported in many cases to remote areas.

The Santa Fe had also tested the #103 FT's and knew the merits of that particular diesel locomotive. East of LaJunta, Colorado, the eastward speed for the #103 was remarkable. When pulling the westward grades between California and Arizona, the diesels were comparable to the latest 2-10-4 steam locomotive models; with one exception, there was no need for water stops.

Recognizing that diesels needed no water stops, ATSF management placed an order. The Santa Fe ordered 68 four-unit sets capable of 5400 horsepower to help with the freight hauling. The idea was to dieselize the desert and mountains divisions between Winslow, Arizona, and Barstow, California.

The Santa Fe, as well as other lines employing the diesels, helped propel product development of the 567 engine to an unprecedented level. Instead of a gradual increase of acceptance of diesel engines, primarily in the form of the 567, the growth was explosive. EMD orders on 567 diesels powered locomotives jumped from 450,00 horsepower in 1941, to 830,000 horsepower in 1942 and topped 117,000,000 horsepower in 1943.

The third occurrence which propelled EMD to the forefront of diesel technology was when the company won the contract to supply diesel engines in the form of the 567 to power LST's (Landing Ship, Tanks). The Navy Bureau of Ships needed power for the 316-foot long, 50-foot wide tank transport. The paired 567 V-12 engines were put to the ultimate test; amphibious assaults ranged from Anzio in the European Theater to Guadalcanal in the Pacific Theater. In all, twenty-one hundred 567 V-12 engines served in over 1000 LST's. After the war, many of the engines were sold to railroads who used them as replacement motors; though one peculiar fact emerged from the resell of the engines -- there was a port and a starboard engine in which one revolved clock-wise, the other counter-clock-wise. Doodlebug "Old Pelican," #M-190, was repowered with a surplus ex-LST V-12 567 prime mover in 1949 as well as other Santa Fe self-propelled cars. The 567 engine proved itself under fire on the rails of the arid and mountainous west and on more than 20 other railroads as well. Coupled with necessity as well as versatility, the 567 prime mover has proved itself for over forty years on America's railroads.

To facilitate the rebuild, the prime mover was completely removed from the frame and rebuilt. Everything from valve springs to cylinder sleeves were replaced. The Cleburne personnel developed an engine cradle which allowed one man to rotate the block in order to have access to the engine at all angles.

The prime mover produced 1500 horsepower as it was delivered in the F7. Discussions early in the rebuild program looked at boosting the horsepower, but a decision was made to keep the horsepower the same and simply go with a complete overhaul. With the combined use of the unit for branch line service and as well as switching, 1500 horsepower was considered sufficient. As an experiment later on in the rebuild program, one CF7, #2452, was equipped with a 645 prime mover which produced an additional 500 horsepower for a total of 2000. After this experiment, a decision was made to stay with the 567 prime mover, partly due to the availability of spare parts within the Santa Fe system.

As part of the safety features, the prime mover would shut down if 72 mph was exceeded; this was slightly higher than the official rating of 65 miles per hour, as posted by EMD. In addition, if the engine exceeded 925 rpm (EMD recommended 800 rpm), the electrical system would shut the engine down as well.

During the rebuild on the unit, the trucks were also removed. The generator and electric traction motors were shipped to San Bernardino, California, to be rewound. The generators were upgraded from D12B to D14, and the traction motors were re-wired from D27 and D37 to D77 specifications. The rewinding represented one of only two jobs not either built or fabricated in the Cleburne Shops. The first batch of CF7's had the trucks painted black, subsequent units had the trucks painted silver and as the first units cycled back to the shops, their trucks were painted silver as well.

The trucks themselves were the very popular Blomberg trucks. This is perhaps the most familiar diesel truck in production. The Blomberg truck had the prominent outside spring hangers which permitted better cushioning for side-to-side-movement. The advantage of the Blomberg truck over other models was the ability to widen the spring base from 56 to 96 inches. EMD likened the truck to a man with his feet apart rather than close together. With the feet apart, the man is harder to push sideways. Consequently, centrifugal force is nullified and the locomotive tilted less on curves. The Blomberg truck was first introduced in 1936, the creation of Martin Blomberg who had joined EMD's staff in a year earlier in 1935. As the units were recycled back through Cleburne for servicing, the trucks were examined for excessive wear and serviced as needed.

The trucks were reassembled upside down for both safety reasons and easy of reassembly. After the traction motors were received from San Bernardino, the reassembly commenced in the up-side-down fashion. After full assembly, two overhead hoists were used to flip the trucks right-side up. The Shop men remembered how visiting school children found this "flipping" to be particularly amusing.

One of the most distinctive features of

ABOVE: CF7's 2645 and 2646 make one of their first appearances in Temple, Texas, on November 6, 1970, fresh from rebuild at Cleburne. Photo by Steve Patterson.

the CF7 locomotive, beside the over-sized cab, is the side sill. The side sill replaced the car body during the rebuild and provided support for the locomotive frame once the car body support was removed and scrapped. The side sill appeared to change as batches of CF7's were finished; some exhibited an open side sill, while other had an enclosed side sill.

The side sill, or referred to in some publications as the fish-belly sill, was manufactured in the Topeka Shop and represents the second and final product not solely fashioned in the Cleburne Shops. Early models utilized an open sill made of Tri-10 steel. Later models used a softer steel and have the sill filled in with gussets to provide additional support. The creation of the side sill represented the most logical solution to the removal of the car-body frame, which caused EMD and GE to pass on the project.

The sill was originally a 24-inch I-beam. A ¾-inch camber was attached to the top of the I-beam and ran the entire length of the frame. This camber was

tapered and thinned as it ran towards the end of the frame. The purpose of the camber was to give additional support for the frame, but to also compensate for the weight of the prime mover. The frame was also strengthened by a dutch plate attached to the inside.

The windows of the CF7 went through several design phases before settling on a final production type. The initial reason for the CF7 was to save the Santa Fe money over the cost of a new unit. With this concern, the old F-unit windows were left in place. This included the crank-style windows left over from the round F-unit cab. Due to feedback from trainmen, who said the windows were much too small for switching, a new style of window was researched. This type of information was solicited over the entire period of the rebuild program by the shop workers. Later units had the slide-mounted windows installed in order to eliminate the complaints from the crewmen regarding the crank-style windows. As the older, crank-style window equipped units made

their way back into Cleburne for servicing, they, too, were equipped with the slide-mounted windows.

The engineers also asked for, and received, a small window near their knee on the engineers side of the cab. This allowed the engineer to look downward at approximately a 45-degree angle to see the brakeman at the front of the locomotive. When bullet-proof glass was mandated, Cleburne replaced the regular window and the small window with one large single piece of glass.

As the program progressed, the Cleburne shop personnel noticed subtle changes from one F-unit to the next which rolled in. The first units kept their original electrical cabinets until the shop personnel noticed the cabinets were not exact in measurements. Some of the cabinets varied from ½ to 1½ inches in dimensions. Because it was not possible to put the same electrical box in the same unit, it was necessary to pre-fabricate the boxes in the Cleburne shops.

The electrical cabinets and wiring

Drawing from <u>Railroad</u>
<u>Model</u> <u>Craftsman</u>,
March 1971, courtesy of
Carstens Publications.

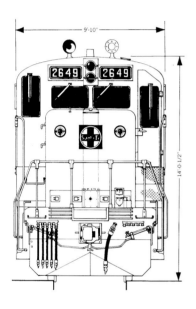

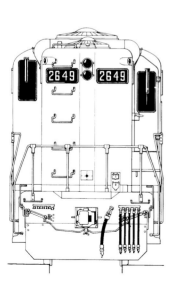

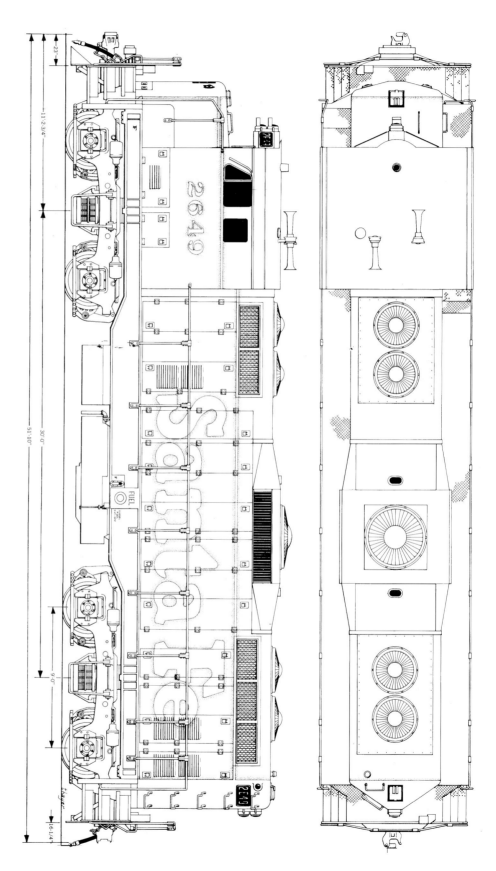

QUOTES & COMMENTS

"The air conditioning in the early units (round cabs) were automobile air conditioners -- you could feel the cold air if you stood 6 inches away from the vent."

"When 2649 first came out of the shops, the cab was so packed with visitors and dignitaries that it made operating the unit difficult. It seems the visitors were fascinated with the air conditioning as he struggled to bring the unit out into the public's eye."

"If one of the units in a consist had an air conditioner, they were switched to the front of the consist... even if they were facing long-hood forward."

"They were uncomfortable to ride in. They kept everything they could from the old locomotives; they even kept the old "toadstool seats" with the small backs from the F-units. I really enjoyed those diesel-hydraulics from Germany; it was like riding in a sports car... but they couldn't pull anything."

"The GP7 was a hundred times better than a CF7. The GP7 would get down and dig; it would pull and pull, and it was quite comfortable to ride in. I operated some of the first GP7's in Texas. We would run all of the newest power here first, then send them off to California as used units, for tax purposes."

"The first CF7's had roll-up windows... just like a car!"

"The EMD's were better pullers, and the GE's were quieter."

"Usually the railroad has two CF7's pull a 50-car train. In another situation, the railroad used 3 CF7's to pull 248 empty cars."

"You've got to realize that early diesels were like steam locomotives -- the hogger ran the locomotive by the seat of his pants; he knew what to do by the feel of the locomotive and the track. The CF7's were just like the F-units in that regard... you felt the track, the slack and all of the engine's vibration. The cabs were noisy, too -- more so than the F's or the GP7's."

"When they built the engines, they didn't put anything in them to cut-out a traction motor. When you get a short in one motor, the whole unit shuts down. Then someone would have to come out and do all kinds of work before you could have the unit on-line again."

"Larry Cena was President at the time. He tried to get the San Bernardino Shop to do the conversion, but they refused. Finally, he talked to Cramer, who said that he could do the job."

"It wasn't designed to be a road engine, and its not safe as a yard engine. It's sluggish, slow to load. The yard/road switch doesn't work and it slips under load. The Santa Fe does nice work, but they should have made the nose longer and the cab shorter. I wouldn't even think of using the commode."

"A friend who is a retired Santa Fe conductor told me the CF7's were the most hated locomotive on the railroad among the people who had to operate them. No one rejoiced more than the train crews when ATSF finally sold them off to sundry short lines and industrials."

"Tell them the drawings are on the outhouse walls!"

ABOVE: ATSF 2509, ex-F7 #224L, photographed at Los Angeles, California, on March 11, 1979, is still sporting its original round cab. Photo taken by Bob Graham, collection of Gordon C. Bassett.

BELOW: A new cab can now be seen on ex-ATSF #2509 at Falcon, Colorado, on May 12, 1986; it is owned by Cadillac & Lake City in this photo, yet still displays full ATSF livery. Compare to photo on page 86 of Florida Northern #50, which is the current owner of ex-ATSF #2509. Photo taken by Ed Fulcomer, collection of Gordon C. Bassett.

ABOVE: ATSF 2489, ex-F7 206C, at Richmond, California, on August 18, 1977. Unit displays many of its as-built features. Photo taken by Peter Arnold, collection of Gordon C. Bassett.

BELOW: Former Santa Fe 2489 at Falcon, Colorado, on October 28, 1986. What a difference a decade makes -- unit has new cab, including a new set of horns and a new air conditioner. Unit also has a new owner -- Colorado & Lake City. More changes are in store for the 2489; it will receive a new coat of blue paint with an outline of Pike's Peak, a new owner (Louisiana & Delta) and a new number (1504). Photo taken by Ed Fulcomer, collection of Gordon C. Bassett.

Major Dimensions

Width:	over side sills	9'-11"
	over cab	9'-10"
	over short hood	4'-3"
	over long hood	5'-0"
	over pilot, max.	10'-0"
Length:	truck centers	30'-0"
	over pilot plates	48'-6"
	over strikers	49'-5"
Height:	over pilot	4'-9"
	over side sill	5'-3"
	over long hood	13'-6"
	over cab roof	14'-5"

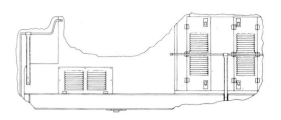

Left side

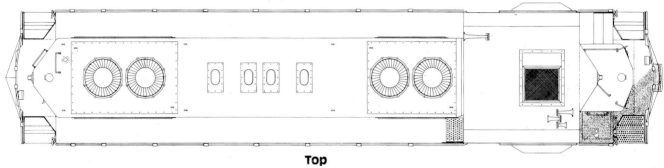

Top

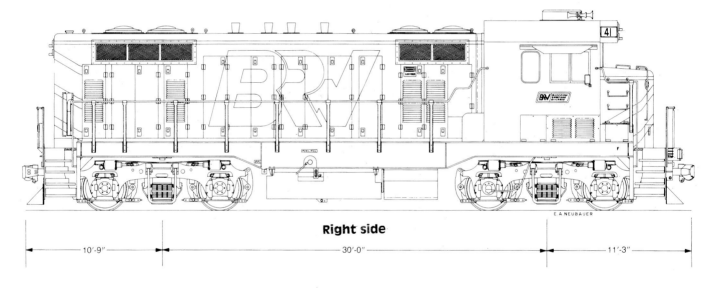

Right side

10'-9"   30'-0"   11'-3"

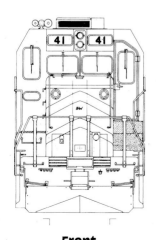

Front

9'-10"

14'-4"

Rear

Drawing from <u>Railroad Model Craftsman</u>, November 1985, courtesy of Carstens Publications.

were brought up to current standards of the early 1970's. One item from the F-unit which was not recycled was the old electrical harness. It was discarded and a new harness was installed. The Cleburne Shop contained several wiring jigs which helped in the manufacture of the wiring bundles and harnesses. It was estimated that there were 4000 electrical terminals that went into each CF7. In addition, each CF7 unit had the capability of m.u.ing with other locomotives utilizing the 27-pin M.U. electrical connection.

The CF7's were equipped with a selector switch which enabled the engineer to choose between switching and road service. When placed in the switch mode, the unit was enabled to load very quickly for switching. Joe Blackwell stated that in that mode the unit "would take right off." In the road service mode, the units loaded more slowly which would help prevent pulling a train apart by breaking a knuckle when starting. As years passed and miles were put on the units, this switch often was the source of unreliability with the locomotive. Many shortlines report that these switches no longer work, and are stuck in the "road service" mode. An older, worn-out switch gear in the electrical cabinet often would not make "transition" from the lower speeds to the higher speeds, usually around 22-24 miles per hour. This would cause the unit to quit loading and the unit would subsequently shut down.

Probably the most confusing aspect of the CF7 program was the round verses angled roof of the cab. The first units emerged from the Cleburne shops sporting a round roof cab. With the rebuild program again designed to save money, it was initially thought by preserving the rounded roof of the F-unit, money could be saved. After the program was well under way, Eldon Whitworth, the Program Coordinator for the project, decided to remove the entire cab unit from the F-unit and replace it with a manufactured cab which had a sharply angled appearance. His decision centered on the fact the short doors placed on the F-unit cab were more costly than the standard-sized doors because they had to be custom fitted. The #2638 is remembered by the shop personnel as being the first re-fitted with the new angled cab. However, several other previously published reports have the #2470 as the first angled cab with the previous 178 units leaving Cleburne with the round cab. As the round cab units made their way back to Cleburne for servicing, they too were refitted with the angled cabs. Some units were sold off by the Santa Fe before being refitted with the angled cabs and continue in service with short lines across the country.

Mr. Whitworth's decision to abandon the round cab led to a confrontation in which his supervisor, C. W. Cramer, had to come to his defense. An official visiting Cleburne felt the decision to abandon the round roof cab was inappropriate and threatened Mr. Whitworth's job. Only by describing the savings in money involving the doors was his job spared and all subsequent CF7's sported the angled cab. Mr. Whitworth remembered that a set of standard replacement doors for a unit ran approximately $600.00. This is approximately half of what custom doors had been running on the round cab models.

One of the big misconceptions regarding the CF7 is the reference to the angled cab as a "Topeka cab." After Lee Townsley instructed the Cleburne Shop members where to cut on the original F-unit, Topeka's guidance on the program was minimal. When Mr. Whitworth made changes to the CF7, they were essentially rubber-stamped by the Topeka Shop, while in essence the work had already been completed and was on the CF7's. In truth, the angled cab was solely a Cleburne creation which can be traced to Eldon Whitworth and had no connection or input from the Topeka Shops. Not only did the idea originate in Cleburne, but the cab was completely manufactured in Cleburne as well.

The large cab allowed a crew of three to be accommodated -- an engineer, fireman and the head brakeman. To allow the crew to view the length of the train, side mirrors were added to both the engineer and brakeman's cab windows. While the engineer mirror was largely in use by most railroads, the addition of the mirror to the brakeman side of the locomotive was a Cleburne Shop innovation which allowed both sides of the train to be monitored by the cab crew.

By converting to the angled cab, the shop personnel were also able to provide the train crew with better sound insulation. A lead plate, as well as foam insulation, was installed in the roof of the cab to deaden noise and vibration. The horn was mounted toward the rear of the cab on early models, but was soon forward of the cab in order to provide comfort and protection to the crew's ears. One shortline, the Washington Central, later relocated the horns to the rear of the long hoods.

The horn, like other parts off of the old F-units, were recycled. A horn off a particular F-unit did not necessarily go on the same frame of the newly rebuilt CF7. The horns were refitted with new diaphragms and were pulled off inventory shelves and utilized as needed. This process meant CF7's left the shop in a variety of horn configurations varying from the single-chime blatt that came off most F-units to 5-chime horns which were utilized on Santa Fe's F3's which operated in passenger service. Later in the rebuild program, as the CF7's came in for subsequent servicing, more modern multi-chime horns were employed on Santa Fe locomotives.

The horn placement and calibration took three months to complete. The decibel level had to be researched, necessitating the Shop personnel to switch locations of the horn as well as add insulation.

In order to mount a radio, a 36-inch square steel plate was mounted to the roof of the locomotive to serve as the ground plane. The plate was held in an elevated horizontal position above the roof by metal legs. This configuration was used because the cab body served as a poor ground plane. The older radios were 12-volt units that were converted to work on a locomotive and had not originally been designed for this purpose. The generators and the air conditioners on the locomotive also created severe interference, thus the need for a separate and isolated ground for the antenna. The steel plate served as a plane to intensify the signal to the antenna and also served to distribute the transmission signal so the range was maximized. The first style of antenna was approximately 6-inches tall by 4-inches. A later model employed a 6-inch whip antenna.

The heaters on the CF7 were mounted to the front wall of the cab. It was noted by shortline operators that the heaters had to be turned on high for heat to be felt by all of the crew members, including the engineer. The heaters were hot water types in which water was heated off of the engine and piped to the front of the cab. Valves regulated the amount of water which followed through the coils and allowed the crew to adjust the temperature control. One shortline engineer, Matt Richie, stated he sometimes had to resort to putting masking tape over the windows to keep cold air from blowing in and negating what little heat was generated from the heaters on his particular units.

The CF7 was equipped with both forward and rear sanders, with two pipes running to each wheel. Each sander box was prefabricated at the shops and held the same approximate volume of sand as did the GP7. While the Santa Fe had sanding stations at most of its diesel service facilities, Gordon Bassett of the Cadillac & Lake City Railroad remembered a different means to replenish sand on a CF7. Without benefit of a sanding tower, he had to drag 80 lb. bags of sand up the steps and pour the sand into the hoppers by hand.

The bell placement represented both a matter of tradition as well as a general lack of space to place it elsewhere on the locomotive. The original placement of the bell on the F7 was under the front pilot of the locomotive. When F-units entered the Cleburne Shops for serving, many shop people noted the units arrived with bells stuffed full of grass and weeds and someone would have to go up under the pilot and remove the debris. Since the Santa Fe determined the short hood of the CF7 would be the front of the locomotive, it was thought the bell had to be mounted on the forward part of the frame. With the short hood being too short to mount a bell and the cab height close to being too tall already, relocation near the original mounting spot seemed the most logical choice. It was deemed the best place would be under the front steps on the engineers side. One shortline, the Mississippi & Skuna Valley Railroad, solved the problem by placing the bell on the brakeman's side, about half way down the top of the long hood. This allowed the bell to be fully heard while switching in either direction, and eliminated the weed problem.

The front pilot of a CF7 contains the only two outward signs the unit was at one time an F-unit. A small section of the anti-climber, approximately 18 inches on either side of the buffer plate, was retained from the F-unit. On the F-unit, the anti-climber ran the full length of the rounded nose, but on the CF7, only the strip adjacent to either side of the buffer plate remained. The second F-unit hold-over was the buffer plate itself which was located directly above the drawbar. These two protrusions left from the frame of the F-unit provided the support required for the front walk-way.

With virtually very part of the F-unit being recycled on the CF7's, the fuel tanks were recycled as well. The first phase of reconstruction involved the emptying and steaming of the fuel tanks. The first units had the tanks mounted under the frame merely by bolts. As these units traveled through the system, the bolts began to work free and a couple of units dropped their tanks onto the tracks. After the problem was discovered, the solution was to bolster the bolts with a fuel rack hanger which prevented the tanks from working loose.

The exhaust stacks on the CF7 evolved as well as the project proceeded. The first 36 units came equipped with a two-stack exhaust system. The system was quickly abandoned due to fires in dry country that resulted from the two stack exhausts. Observers noted the two stack system emitted a dual red line of carbon sparks when the CF7's were under full throttle. Of the 36 units that had a two-exhaust stack system, all but about a dozen were converted to the four stack system

when they cycled back through Cleburne on scheduled service stops.

To correct the problem, the Cleburne personnel purchased the original four-stack exhaust system from Farr Manufacturing. The Cleburne personnel then built a close copy for only a third of the original purchase price. From then on out, all four stack exhaust boxes were built in the Cleburne shops.

The original spark arrestors were built in the Cleburne Shops and made for a distinctive protrusion above the long hood. The spark arrestors, coupled with the two stack exhaust system, were considered ineffective and were ultimately eliminated.

With the F-unit carbody being taken down to the frame, the Cleburne personnel had to manufacture a new control stand for the CF7. The new control stand was completely manufactured in the Cleburne shops and was modeled after the GP7 control stand. Since the Santa Fe designated the short hood as the front, the control stand was fashioned as such. With the arrival of the CF7, many railroads were still utilizing Alco switchers and comparisons were soon made. Controls on a CF7 were hard to work in the back-up mode because the engineer had to look through the rear view mirror, versus swiveling their chair around as they could on Alco and EMD switchers. Most of these comparisons took place before the advent of radio packsets and it was rumored many rear-view mirrors were smashed out of anger on the engineer's side by a mad hogger who either had his hand signals missed or missed the signals of his brakeman.

The Santa Fe bragged that it was the first railroad in the country to equip its locomotives with air conditioning. It was often thought the first CF7's, units #2649 through #2579, did not come equipped with air conditioning. When presented with this suggestion, the men of the Cleburne Shops were emphatic in their belief all CF7's were equipped as such from the start of the rebuild program. These particular units employed a Dallas-built Mark IV air conditioner which hung inside the cab, crossway above the front windshield. The air conditioner unit had a compressor which was powered by an air compressor shaft. However, as these units were recycled back through Cleburne, the angled cab was installed and they were refitted with the boxy exterior type of air conditioner found on later CF7's.

Vapor and Prime Corporations were used to manufacture the air conditioning units which went on the angled cabs. The flat roof of the angled cab housed the air conditioning, along with the horn and the antenna. In designing the height of the angled cab, the Cleburne personnel had to

have measurements taken of the LaJunta, Colorado, roundhouse, which represented the shortest height on stall doors on the Santa Fe system.

The CF7 program also served as an experiment for the Santa Fe on the practicality of air conditioning in diesel locomotives. James Parker, an engineer who was based out of Cleburne, remembered when the #2649 first came out of the shops, the cab was so packed with visitors and dignitaries that it made operating the unit difficult. It seems the visitors were fascinated with the air conditioning as he struggled to bring the unit out into the public's eye. He further stated "the crew felt if they could monitor the air (environment) inside the cab, it would have a positive effect on the electrical boxes which were also located in the cab." Their rationale was that "if moisture could be blocked out on humid days and dust and dirt could be controlled on warm days, the electrical leads in the electrical panel would fare better than non-air conditioned units." One of the chronic problems with the 200-series F-units was that the electrical leads and contacts in the electrical cabinet would become fouled by dirt and dust. Besides the basic crew comfort factor, the Santa Fe actually improved its locomotive reliability and performance by adapting the crew's suggestion of adding air conditioning.

When the carbody frame of the F-unit was removed, there was a mild concern regarding the lack of weight on the CF7. In order to make adjustments, some additional weight was added to the rear of the CF7. The first three units were ballasted to make sure the rebuilt units were of the same approximate weight as the F-units. After the first three, the other units were not ballasted.

Later one of the problems associated with the CF7 locomotive in switching centered on its tendency to literally spin its wheels under a heavy load. It was a simple matter of too much power on a light switching unit. Mr. Slater of the LAJ stated his units "rode better than their Alco S2's and S4's, but were very slippery and didn't hold the rails as well as the Alco switchers."

The brakes, along with the rest of the truck, were rebuilt. The brakes were upgraded from 24-RL to 26L on most units as they cycled back through. The 26L brakes brakes were known to be easier to work and much easier to maintain.

In addition, a new air plate was developed in the Cleburne shops by two employees, Wiley and Sinclair. The air plate served as the mount for all air equipment and when an application for air was applied, the application was transferred through the plate to all contacts and then

BELOW: ATSF 2606 soaks up the California sunshine with sister unit 2642 in background, at Stockton on September 18, 1983. Both units were built early in the program with round cabs, but later received angled cabs at Cleburne. Photograph by Jay Reed.

to the brakes. The air plate was mounted to a ½-inch steel plate, slid into place under the cab and welded into place. Next, the cab was lowered into place and mounted on top of the air plate assembly. Once the air plate was mounted, subsequent repairs could be done from the outside by accessing a panel below the cab.

Since the CF7 was intended to be a multi-purpose locomotive, a shortcoming on the switching side was discovered early on in the rebuild program. This problem was noted on the LAJ CF7's in which the crews noticed the units had a tendency of "picking up" or binding the wheels when stopping, resulting in flat spots on the wheels. The problem was caused by the clasp brake shoes and were soon replaced by the Santa Fe. This replacement resulted in preventing flat spots, but it also provided for longer stopping distances.

One of the little known features on the CF7 was the crew comfort station. Each of 233 units had a station built into the locomotive for the comfort of the crew. The first two units, #2649 and #2648 had "chute" toilets which allowed waste to be dumped directly on the tracks. After this experiment, all other units employed the chemical holding tanks. The station was moved from the rear of the F-unit to the short front hood of the CF7. In noting the short hood on a CF7 is exceedingly short, the shop personnel cut through the deck plating in order to place the commode in this very short nose. The crew stepped down three steps to enter the comfort station. John Campbell, a volunteer with the Kentucky Railway Museum, which has the distinction of being the first museum to preserve a CF7, wrote this in regard to accessing the entrance door to the comfort

station...he said it was a maneuver in which a crewman was "turning around, stepping down, ducking your head and twirling, all in the same movement." Joe Blackwell, an engineer with BNSF, remembered the CF7 being a good switch engine; however, he had reservations regarding the comfort station when he said, "They were extra bad in the home-chopped units because the entrance door was still at cab floor level, but only three feet high, making it very difficult, as well as unsafe to enter." Crew members seldom used the facility due to the hassle of entering and exiting the short hood door. If a crew member was sitting on the commode, he had the front truck and its blower motors directly to the his right. To his immediate left was the sanders and the skin of the short hood. Most crew members said the term "cramped" was an understatement.

Besides the side sills and large cab, the short and long hood on the CF7 were also very distinctive. Some have gone as far as attempting to describe a CF7 as a locomotive with a GE short hood and an EMD long hood. Whatever the call, the short and long hood both posed initial problems for the Cleburne Shop personnel.

The short hood was essentially a customized piece on each CF7. After the F-unit was cut down, the space where the traditional short hood should have gone was only half of the normal space on a GP7. The shop crews fabricated the short hood around the collision posts. In order to develop protection for the crew in the event of an accident, 8-inch steel I-beams were mounted vertically to the frame. To form a connecting web to the I-beams, ½-inch wall tubing was welded to the posts. The short hood was then shaped around the collision posts.

After the #2649, all long hoods were manufactured in the Cleburne shops. Two jigs were developed to manufacture the hood in the Boiler Shop. When the long hood left the shop, it contained all the electrical connections needed, including cooling fans. The hood simply needed to be lowered on the CF7 frame and the connections made.

One of the specialties of the Cleburne Shops was its ability to have skilled men and women prefabricate many of the parts which went into the CF7 rebuild program. With the exception of the side sills, which were made in Topeka, Kansas, and the traction motor/generator being rebuilt in San Bernardino, California, all other parts were developed, built and installed at the Cleburne Shops. Most of the parts were kept in stock and as a craft needed a particular part, they simply took the needed item from inventory.

The workers of the Santa Fe at Cleburne contributed enormously to the program in the sense their craftsmanship resulted in lower costs to the railroad. Examples are engine cradle, the air plate design and even the simple fact the personnel believed that the rebuild program would work to begin with.

In researching the CF7 program, it became immediately apparent to me that few schematic or mechanical drawings existed of the program. Mr. Cramer was even informed that management from the Santa Fe wanted to see drawings for the CF7 project. When prodded to produce the drawings, his response was simple, yet typical of his way of conducting business out of the Cleburne Shops; "Tell them the drawings are on the outhouse walls."

Two notable exceptions would be schematics for the electrical and pipefitting personnel. Eldon Whitworth, the Program

Coordinator, noted that a spiral notebook was kept on the first few units, but eventually the men knew what was needed to be added to the next unit. The CF7's were also rebuilt in what was referred as batches. Within each batch were subtle changes from one CF7 to the next. This craftsmanship resulted in what was essentially a hand-built locomotive. The Cleburne rebuild program was not an all-male domain either, with at least one woman working in the electrical craft and another in the boilermaker craft.

The CF7 locomotives could be found over much of the Santa Fe system. Many served as switchers, performed local worked and even worked coupled to other locomotives hauling mainline freight. One particular job that fell to the CF7 was working the potash trains out of Carlsbad, New Mexico.

The Carlsbad to Clovis, New Mexico, run was noted for having heavy drags of potash trains running between the two communities. In the early 1970's, Santa Fe began converting 200-series cabless F-units for slug work on the potash trains. The units looked externally like an F-unit, but had the portholes, stacks, fans and fuel tanks removed. The electrical cabinets were retained, but concrete was put in place of the prime movers. The slugs were to be mated to other operating F-units, but the conversion project ceased when CF7's were made available. CF7's #2612-2625, fourteen in all, were mated to the slugs for work on the potash trains and were equipped with RCE. A typical train would involve two to three sets of mated CF7's and slugs. The slugs would cut out automatically at 30 miles per hour.

New slugs were built and replaced the F-units, but retained the F-units old numbers. Later, GP7's replaced the CF7's, which returned to service on the entire system. A redesigned system into Carlsbad in the early 1980's allowed for the discontinuation of the slug service.

The proposed SPSF merger brought a new paint scheme, red and yellow, to the Santa Fe, but not to the CF7's. With the proposed merger, the Santa Fe had contingency plans as of October 10, 1985, to renumber the remaining 132 CF7's from the 2417-2649 series to the 1000-1131 series. However, after the merger was called off, the plan to renumber the units was scrapped and the CF7's proceeded to be sold off to shortlines. No CF7 received the SPSF red and yellow paint scheme.

ABOVE: Four CF7 slug sets on train 2330 at Getty Wye on the Carlsbad Industrial Spur, May 9, 1974. The train is enroute from the Duval Corporation mine and is shown here waiting for an opposing train. Photo by Joe McMillan.

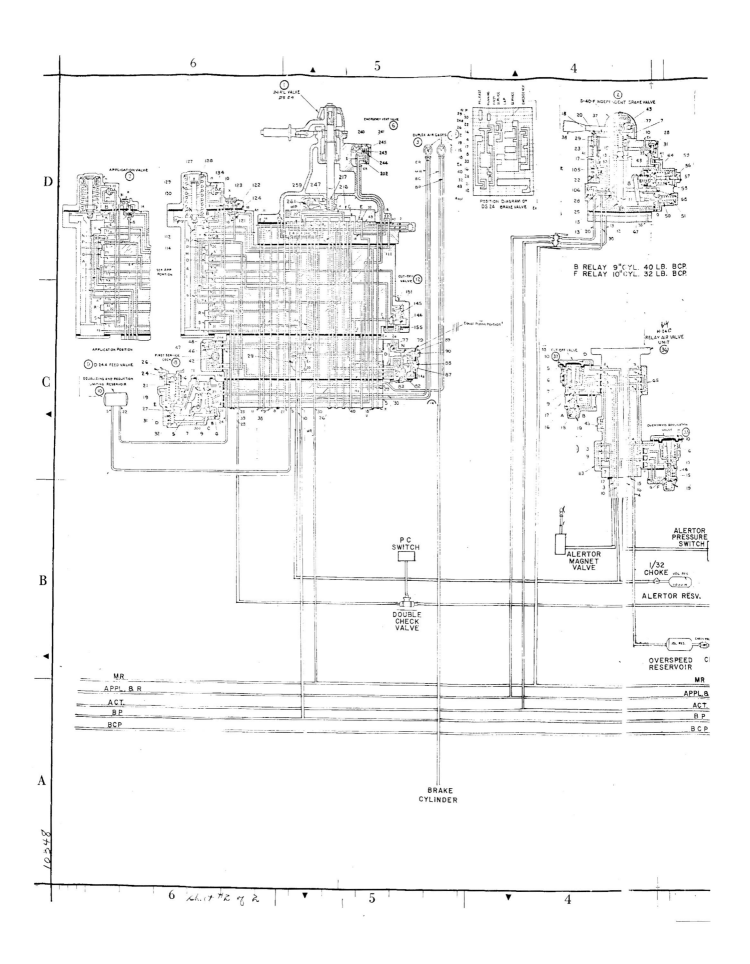

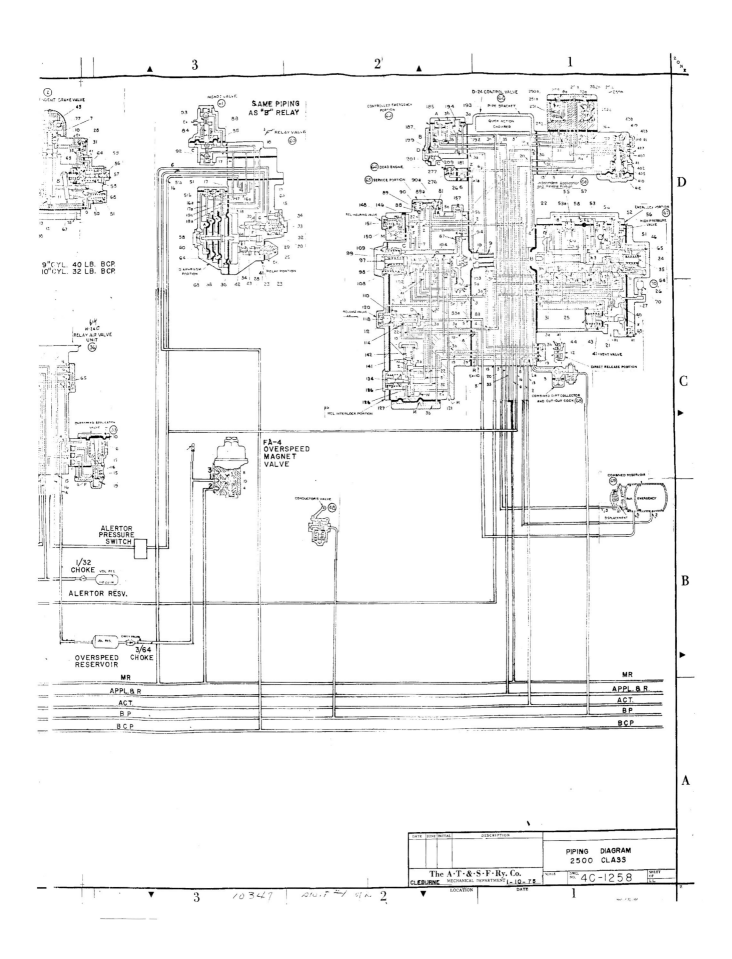

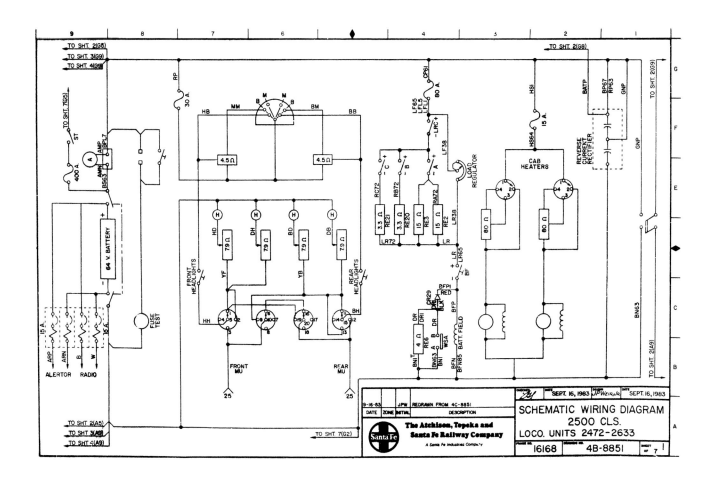

SCHEMATIC WIRING DIAGRAM
2500 CLS.
LOCO. UNITS 2472-2633

The Atchison, Topeka and Santa Fe Railway Company

A Santa Fe Industries Company

FRAME NO.	DRAWING NO.	SHEET
16168	4B-8851	1 of 7

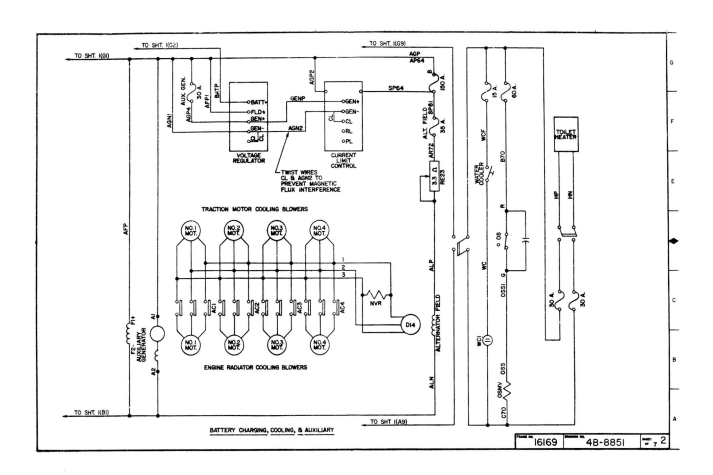

BATTERY CHARGING, COOLING, & AUXILIARY

FRAME NO.	DRAWING NO.	SHEET
16169	4B-8851	2 of 7

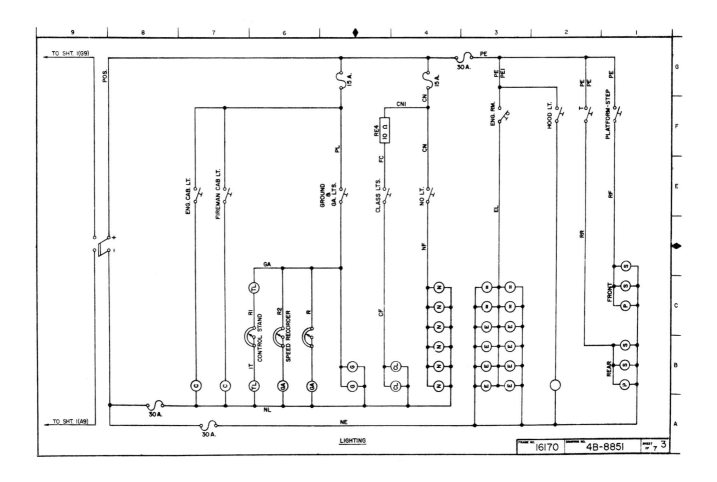

LIGHTING

FRAME NO.	DRAWING NO.	SHEET
16170	4B-8851	3 of 7

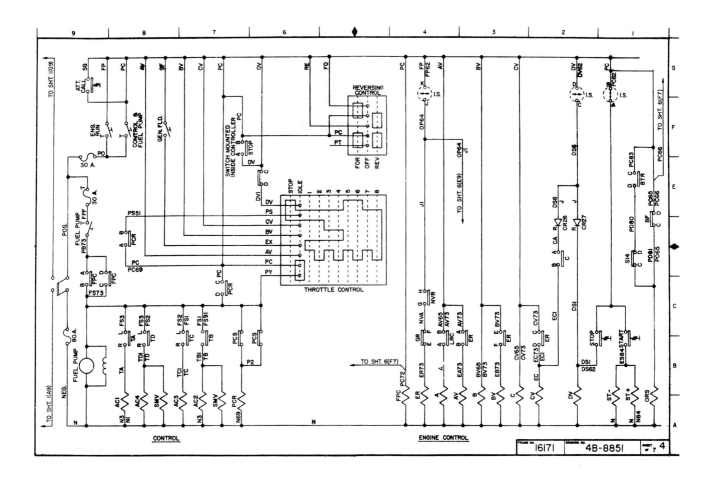

CONTROL   ENGINE CONTROL

FRAME NO.	DRAWING NO.	SHEET
16171	4B-8851	4 of 7

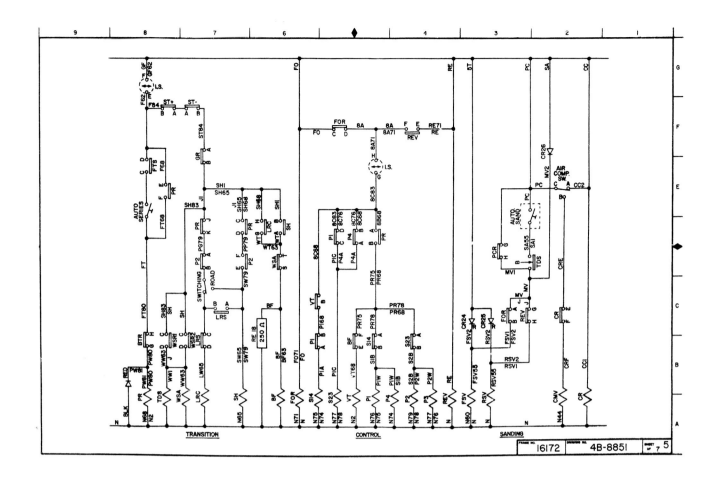

			M. U. RECEPTACLE
	1		SPARE
	2	SG	SIGNAL
	3	DV	ENGINE SPEED
	4	N	CONTROL NEGATIVE
	5	ES	EMERGENCY SANDING
	6	GF	GENERATOR FIELD
	7	CV	ENGINE SPEED
	8	FO	LOCO. DIRECTION
	9	RE	LOCO. DIRECTION
	10	WS	WHEEL SLIP
	11		SPARE
	12	BV	ENGINE SPEED
	13	PC/FP	POS. CONTROL/FUEL PUMP
	14	SN	EXCITATION SET UP
	15	AV	ENGINE SPEED
	16	ER	ENGINE RUN
	17	B	*DYNAMIC BRAKE
	18		SPARE
	19	NN	NEGATIVE
	20	BW	*BRAKE WARNING
	21	BG	*DYNAMIC BRAKE
	22	CC	COMPRESSOR SYN.
	23	SA	AUTO. SAND
	24	BC/PRC	BRAKE CONTROL
	25	HL	M. U. HEADLIGHT
	26	SV	SPARE
	27		SPARE

* CONNECTED BETWEEN RECEPTACLES ONLY

REVERSE 8 & 9 FROM SHORT HOOD END
AT 120 POINT T.B.

XF-PIN 25-SHORT HOOD END

LONG HOOD END

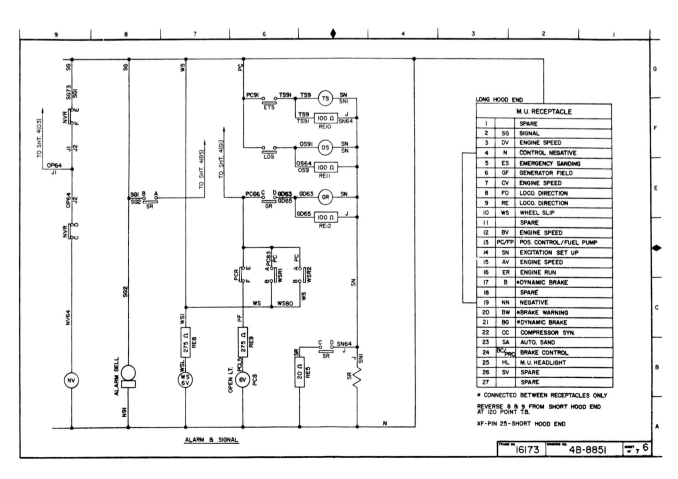

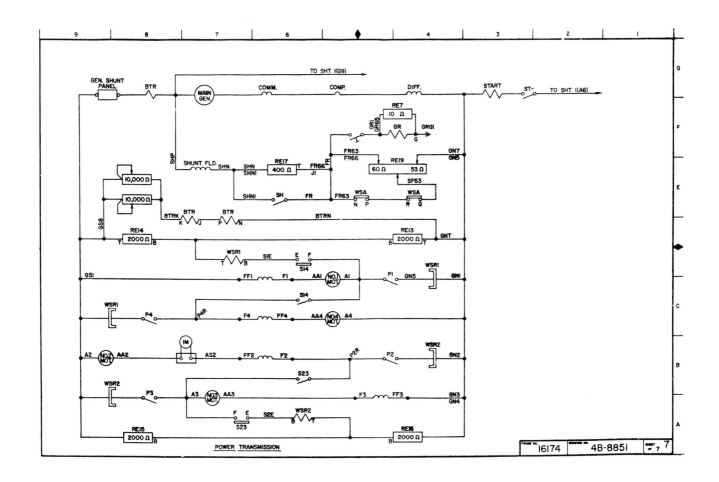

BELOW: Newspaper article which marked the completion of the CF7 program from the scrapbook of Eldon Whitworth.

CF-7 locomotive conversion project is completed

UNIT NUMBER 2417, LAST OF THE CF-7S, CAME off the line at Cleburne shop March 15, marking the end of one of the more notable locomotive conversion projects on the Santa Fe—and possibly in the railroad industry.

Eight years before, almost to the day—March 13, 1970—the first CF-7 unit, Number 2649, was unveiled in a ceremony at the shop. In all, Cleburne shop has produced 233 of the CF-7 units.

Santa Fe brought old 200-class F-7 diesel units with the older "streamline" body construction into the shop, where Cleburne personnel transformed them into sleek new dual-purpose locomotives for both road and switching service, with a finishing touch of the bright blue and yellow Santa Fe paint scheme.

The conversion program was based on sound economics. The units were transformed for about 40 per cent of the cost of new locomotives of comparable (1,500) horsepower.

The CF-7 program ended simply because there are no more 200-class A units left to convert, C. W. Cramer, superintendent of shops, explained.

"I'm sorry to see the program over," Cramer said, with a touch of sentiment. "It's been a great thing for Santa Fe, saving the company a lot of money, and a great thing for our people here at Cleburne."

Cramer pointed out that other conversion programs, such as the GP-7 and GP-9 low profile unit projects already in progress, will provide a smooth transition to keep the shop work forces busy.

Posing with pride in front of the last CF-7 to roll off the line at Cleburne shop are, from left, Eldon Whitworth, assistant general foreman; L. C. Stewart and W. C. Akey, boilermakers; Charles W. Cramer, superintendent of shops; C. A. Moser, assistant superintendent-locomotives, and Frank H. Bowles, general foreman.

KEY FOR AERIAL VIEW OF SHOPS

1	Air Brake Facility
2	Boiler Shop
3	Car Shops
4	Lube Facility
5	Machine Shop
6	Maintenance Office
7	North End Paint Shop
8	Planing Mill & Electricians Shop
9	Power House
10	Ramp Engine Service Facility
11	Roundhouse Site
12	South End Paint Shop
13	Steel Car Repair Shop
14	Store Department
15	Truck Shop
16	Wash Rack
17	Wheel Shop

Santa Fe's Cleburne Shops

Mr. C. W. Cramer started his career with the Santa Fe Railroad as an elevator operator in the Chicago corporate office. After this stint, he was assigned to the electrical department where he spent the typical four years as an apprentice. After completing his apprenticeship, he was assigned as an ASDE (Assistance Supervisor of Diesel Engines). He came to Cleburne Shops as General Foreman over the Ramp (Running Repair). He was promoted to General Foreman of the Back Shop. His last assignment, which ran until his retirement, was the Superintendent of Shops for Cleburne. Photo collection of Eldon Whitworth.

BELOW: Aerial view of Santa Fe's Cleburne Shops. View is looking from the south. Courtesy of W.F. Stepp.

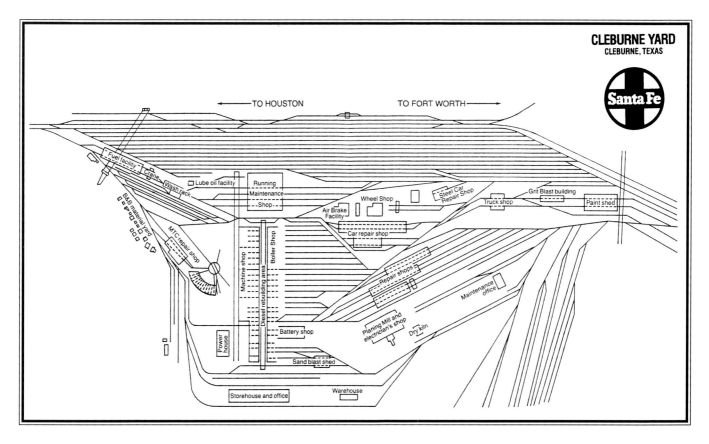

ABOVE: Track layout at Cleburne. Courtesy of Cleburne Shop Reunion.

BELOW: Close-up view of the new style of cut lever which allowed crews to "pull the pin" from either side of the locomotive. Polaroid photo from Cleburne Shops, collection of Eldon Whitworth.

Work-In-Progress Inside the Cleburne Shops

LEFT: The engine block was removed from the F-units and this cradle allowed the prime mover to be rotated for easier access. All of the CF7's had their prime movers completely rebuilt at Cleburne in this fashion. Polaroid taken by shop personnel, collection of Eldon Whitworth.

RIGHT: This view shows exhaust stacks being rebuilt The CF7's originally left Cleburne with two exhaust stacks, but later emerged from the Shops with four. Polaroid taken by shopworker at Cleburne, collection of Eldon Whitworth.

THIS PAGE: Two views of work-in-progress in the Cleburne Shop. Note the four-stack arrangement which is clearly visible in each photo. It is also easy to recognize 16 cylinders in each of the 567 prime movers. The unit in the top photo is devoid of wheels, while the bottom CF7 has the shiniest trucks and wheels that I've ever seen. From looking at the placards placed about, it appears that 2473 is available for inspection. Look at the spotless and uncluttered work area, as well. Collection of Allen R. Johnson.

LEFT: Unique view of 2649, the first CF7, early in the process of being built. The F-unit contours are evident in the cab roof and windows. Notice metal plates welded to collision posts. Gaps will be filled and smoothed-over by sanding to hide and reinforce the seams. Pilot retains buffer plate and part of the anti-climber from the F-unit. Note open frame design and lack of number board-headlight assembly. Also, prime mover has not yet been installed. Photo by John B. McCall.

ABOVE: Now, the 2649 is little further along in the rebuild. The cab and nose has been painted, the prime mover has been installed, and accessories like the coupler, handrails, m.u. cables, along with the stand, and some glass have all been added. Photo by John B. McCall.

RIGHT: Overhead view highlights the 2646 (fourth CF7) in a later stage of assembly. Headlights, number boards and front door have all been added. Cleburne Shop forces will fabricate the long hood that will soon house the 2646's prime mover. Collection of Allen R. Johnson.

The Shops

The Cleburne Shop facility was, and is still today, an impressive facility. The Roundhouse was constructed in 1900 and contained 36 stalls at its zenith. The Roundhouse was constructed of white limestone which was mined in Johnson County, Texas. The turntable that served to place the locomotives in the stalls was 120 feet in length.

The Machine Shop and Boiler Shop are two parallel buildings which are serviced by a transfer table which ran between both buildings. The Machine Shop held 23 stalls and was 515-feet long, 124-feet deep, with a ceiling height of 75 feet. It was constructed in 1926 by H. D. McCoy of Cleburne, Texas. The Shop originally contained 45 different machines which could turn out parts for locomotives. Included with the various machines was a 240 ton-rated Whiting engine hoist which could move items up and down the 23 stalls. This overhead crane was constructed in 1922.

The Machine Shop housed virtually every piece of metal-working machine which could be found. Included in the extensive list were lathes of all sizes, milling machines, drill presses and boring mills.

The Boiler Shop was the same as the Machine Shop, 515-feet in length, but contained only 16 stalls. It was erected when the Machine Shop was built in 1926, also by H. D. McCoy. The building was made of reinforced concrete and steel. This facility replaced an earlier building which had been constructed in 1900 when Cleburne was first awarded the repair facility.

The Blacksmith Shop, heavily used in the days of steam, contained a 5000 psi steam hammer. The foundation of the steam hammer was embedded 30-feet deep in the ground. This hammer had the capacity to cut steel 24-inches thick. In addition, forges, blowers, anvils and welding equipment were also located in the building.

The Powerhouse contained three 500-horsepower boilers at the time of the closing of the facility. A previous structure housed 4 boilers which were rated at 300 horsepower each. The power generated by the Powerhouse was either used to produce electricity or to generate compressed air.

The Smokestack, constructed in 1929, is one of the most recognizable landmarks in Cleburne. The stack rises over the city to a height of 230 feet, not including an additional 17 feet which are underground and serves as the foundation. The stack base is 14-feet thick in diameter and 7-feet thick at the top.

The Coach Shop had the capacity to handle 250 coaches per year. This shop was parallel to the Machine and Boiler Shops. Running from north to south through the yard, you first encounter the Coach Shop, then the Boiler Shop and on the southern end of the yard was the Machine Shop. The Coach Shop served as one of two facilities utilized in the CF7 rebuild program.

The Coach Shop was housed in a large brick building. Tracks and facilities

BELOW: Cleburne's new Machine Shop, photographed on March 11, 1931. Note the transfer table to serve the 23 doors of the shop. Photo courtesy of the Kansas State Historical Society.

BELOW: Santa Fe's new Blacksmith Shop and Boiler Shop on left, and new Machine Shop on right, photographed on March 11, 1931. Photo courtesy of the Kansas State Historical Society.

were sufficient to allow 26 coaches to be served simultaneously. All crafts needed to completely overhaul a coach could be found working under this roof, including carpenters, cabinet workers, sash and door men, glaziers, upholsterers and painters. The Coach Shop was destroyed by fire on September 23, 1976, at 11:20 p.m. Many residents and employees remember the spectacular fire which resulted in the total loss of the Coach Shop. Barrels of paint, thinner and other highly flammable liquids were consumed and added to the brilliant fire. Witnesses said containers shot hundreds of feet into the air as the liquids caught fire.

To handle the huge amounts of lumber required to run the railroad, a Mill Shop was built for the Gulf, Colorado and Santa Fe Railroad. At full capacity, and with plenty of pine and other timber from east Texas, the Mill Shop could handle 600,000 board feet per month. A modern dry kiln helped to provide for the voracious appetite for wood of the Coach and Freight Car Shops.

The Diesel Shop was located on the southern end of the yard and was a recent addition to the Cleburne Shops, having been constructed in 1979. After the Santa Fe dieselized, the shop helped in servicing the 494 diesel units which were assigned to Cleburne for scheduled maintenance.

The Cleburne Shop was primarily a steam repair shop as far as locomotives went, until 1945. In that year, several Class 100 diesels were transferred to Bellville Yard (near Houston). Personnel from Winslow Yard were transferred to help with the maintenance of the diesels. The diesel serving ramps were almost an afterthought. Box car roofs and other scrap materials were used to piecemeal a diesel service area. The crude arrangement lasted from 1945 when the diesels were transferred in until 1979, when a new facility was constructed on the south end of the yard.

The Store Department was located on the eastern portion of the yard and was housed in a two-story reinforced concrete and brick structure which served as the inventory supply center for the yard. At its peak of operation, the Cleburne Shops stocked an estimated 83,000 different items, for a total of 3,300,000 items in inventory. Many of the shop-fashioned items for the CF7 rebuild program were inventoried and stored here for future use. The Storehouse was 60-feet deep and 662-feet in length. This facility replaced an earlier building which was 38-feet deep and 200-feet long and had been constructed in 1916.

The Paint Shop handled approximately 75 cars a year. This particular facility

was located on the extreme northern end of the yard.

The Freight Car Repair facility was located north of the Coach Shop and occupied the largest space of any of the shops at Cleburne. Complete repairs could be undertaken to return cars back to revenue service as quickly as possible. The Mill Shop supplied lumber to repair the sides, roofs and flooring of the box cars. Full air-brake equipment repairs could also be handled by the shop.

With the need to supply steam locomotives with water, 12 wells were dug over the course of the years. One well even hit oil, but Galveston mandated the well be was capped because the Santa Fe needed water, not oil. Towards the end of the Shop's operations, 3 wells were still active.

While many railroad shops had a single specialty such as locomotive repair, or car repair, the Cleburne Shops represented a complete and comprehensive repair facility. Work could be conducted on freight cars, passenger coaches and the shops successfully made the conversion from steam repair to diesel repair.

At its height of production, the Cleburne Shops employed 1500 men and women. The effect on the local economy was understandably great. The impact of the closing of the Cleburne Shops was felt just as much.

ABOVE: Santa Fe CF7 #2645, the fifth CF7 produced, exhibits many of the characteristics of the early CF7's, including the navy paint with yellow trim, open frame, two stacks with the gigantic spark arrestors, crank-style cab windows from the F-units, black trucks and a pair of "blatt" horns. Note that the step edges are not yellow; this was added to later units. Also note the ACI (Automatic Car Identification) label on the sideframe right below the "S". Emporia, Kansas, November 1973.

BELOW: Rear view of 2645. Note the absence of number boards on the rear of the unit; 2649 was the only CF7 built with number boards on both the front and rear, because its long hood came from a wrecked GP7B.

BELOW: Fireman's side view of 2591, decked out in Santa Fe's new Warbonnet paint scheme in November 1973 at Emporia, Kansas. Notice the fireman's rear view mirror (longer than the engineer's side, too!).

BOTTOM: Engineer's side view. The 2591 has newer cab windows and a closed (also known as "boxed") frame, and four stacks instead of two, but still sports those huge barn-like spark arrestors. Notice F-unit in background with same type of arrestors. Also note that one of the cab windows is permanently shut, while the other can slide open.
All photos these two pages taken by C. H. Humphreys, collection of Steve Hottle.

"Charlie's Stump"

After the Hurricane of 1900, a large tree stump washed ashore at Galveston. This stump was to become the centerpiece of local folklore which persists today around Cleburne, Texas.

The stump was brought to Cleburne to be used by coppersmiths to hammer out sheets of copper. The surface of the stump had enough "give" to where the hammer when striking the copper would not break though the sheet. The Copper Shop was a part of the Boiler Shop, and this is where the general forging and hammering of metals took place. It was within these facilities that the majority of steam locomotive repair took place.

The stump came to C. W. Cramer's attention, who admired its contribution to the work force and the history behind it. As with the steam locomotive repair, forging and hammering of metals for the CF7's was also done using "the stump." It was generally known that Cramer wanted to privately obtain the stump after his retirement. In preparation for the retirement event, the stump was removed from the Copper Shop and placed out of the way in storage at the Coach Shop. On September 23, 1976, a fire alarm was set off at 11:20 p.m. as flames totally engulfed

the Coach Shop and the entire facility was destroyed. The fire was accelerated due to stored barrels of paint, thinners, and other flammables. Amazingly, the next morning the stump was found to have survived the blaze. Cramer had assigned a shop employee to watch over the stump with a fire hose and douse any sparks or hot spots that might have flared. Knowing Mr. Cramer put such stock in the stump, it was sandblasted and refurbished by the Shop personnel. The fire had caused the stump to crack, therefore two iron hoops were fastened around both the top and base. A metal base was created for the stump to rest upon. The stump, for whatever reason, was next assigned to the Store Department, where salvage items would be put up for sale. While visiting the Store Department, Shopman J. D. Williams noticed the stump and purchased it for its salvage value. Through the grapevine, Cramer heard of the purchase and persuaded Williams to re-sell him the stump. The shop personnel who told the story were not aware of any monetary details, but knew that "Cramer got his stump back."

The stump first went north of Cleburne in 1980 to Joshua, Texas,

Cramer's residence at the announcement of his retirement. It stayed at his residence until his death in 1989. Upon his death, the stump was moved south to Rio Vista, Texas, by men of the Cleburne Shops and positioned as a monument to Charles W. Cramer. A simple metal plaque titled "Charlie's Stump" details the travels of the stump and what it meant to Mr. Cramer. The stump sits in a small park between the local post office and the cowpasture bank. The bank received its moniker because of the grassy field used by local ranchers to fly in, conduct bank business and then to fly out. The bank and field are complete with windsock to let the pilots know of the wind conditions.

Every shop person interviewed for this book spoke highly of Charles W. Cramer, with no exceptions. Mr. Cramer was referred to as simply Mr. Cramer on the job; however, on other informal occasions, such as fishing trips, he could be called Charlie. Even in the car on the way to a wreck site, he was Charlie, but once he started the supervision of the wreck, he was instantly known as Mr. Charles Cramer. The men knew their role around him, respected him, and certainly mourned his passing.

CHARLIE'S STUMP

WASHED ASHORE INTO THE SANTA FE RAILROAD SHOP AREA ON GALVESTON ISLAND DURING THE DEVASTATING 1900 HURRICANE. IT REMAINED THERE UNTIL IT WAS TO BE DESTROYED DURING A CLEAN UP EFFORT.

SPARED AND MOVED BY RAIL TO THE SANTA FE RAILROAD SHOPS IN CLEBURNE, USED THERE AS A SURFACE FOR SHAPING AND FORMING STEAM ENGINE PARTS IN THE BUSY SHOPS.

MOVING TO MEET A NEW CHALLENGE IN THE EARLY 1950'S, THE CLEBURNE SHOP OF 1800 WORKERS BEGAN CONVERTING STEAM ENGINES TO DIESEL. SEVERELY DAMAGED IN 1976 FIRE OF THE COACH SHOP BUT AGAIN ESCAPED UNDER THE PROTECTION OF "THE RAILROADERS."

REFINISHED AND PRESENTED TO RETIRING, C.W. "CHARLIE" CRAMER, SUPERINTENDENT OF CLEBURNE'S SANTA FE SHOPS, AND ITS MOST DEDICATED PROTECTOR. REMAINING WITH HIM FROM 1980 UNTIL HIS DEATH IN 1989.

RESTORED ONCE AGAIN AND PLACED HERE IN 1993 BY LOCAL CO-WORKERS, AS A MEMORIAL TO THE SANTA FE SHOPS IN CLEBURNE, AND TO THE MAN
KNOWN THROUGHOUT THE RAILROAD WORLD AS
"MR. SANTA FE", CHARLIE CRAMER.

Photo by Cary F. Poole.

Other Cleburne Rebuilds

While the Cleburne rebuild program consisted of a complete rebuild of the locomotive, it was not the first massive rebuild program conducted. That credit goes to the Paducah-based program which was orchestrated by the Illinois Central Railroad in the 1960's. By the mid-1960's, the Illinois Central found itself with a fleet of 396 GP7/9's, most with an excess of 15 years of service on them. The IC looked at purchasing higher horsepower locomotives, but determined that 1750 horsepower Geeps would still be ideal over its relatively level terrain.

By 1967, the IC had decided the Paducah, Kentucky, shop could handle a complete in-house rebuild and commenced with the program to rebuild both switchers and road units. Initial studies demonstrated that another 12-15 years of service could be obtained from a rebuilt unit which would be refurbished at half the cost of a new unit.

The first unit was an SW7 which emerged from the shop with an unaltered appearance, but with a new electrical harness, complete mechanical upgrade and an upgrade on the braking system. Geep #9109 emerged in June 1967 from the shop and made its public debut by running through a banner stretched across the tracks which read, "Better Than Ever." This unit was mechanically rebuilt, but retained its original high-nose appearance. A Paducah Shop trademark began with this unit; a rebuilt unit would be released with a new road number which dropped by 1000. Thus the 9109 became the 8109.

In March 1968, the Shop adopted the practice of chopping the noses along with the complete mechanical rebuild as on earlier rebuilds. The Shop achieved the nose-lowering by cutting out the sides of the high nose and re-welding the nose roof back to the lowered sides. This created a lower nose, but not a sloped nose found on EMD designed low-nose GP9's.

Another distinctive feature which easily points to a Paducah-rebuild is an ox-yoke shaped housing which rests just to the rear of the cab on the long hood. The ox-yoke attachment is the housing for the paper air filters and are located over the blower assembly. An additional feature from Paducah was the application of "frog-eye" headlights which were mounted side-by-side on the low nose. With the exception of the chopped nose and air filter boxes, the units retained their basic EMD shape. The mechanical rebuild improved

the units and were labeled as GP8's from GP7's and GP10's from GP9's. The Illinois Central Railroad was so pleased with the rebuild program that they began to purchase used Geeps from other railroads to rebuild. The railroad even joined forces with Precision National Corporation to rebuild locomotives of this nature for other lines. Today, VMV Enterprises operates the facility and rebuilds locomotives for the current used locomotive market.

After the CF7 rebuild program, the Cleburne Shops hosted the GP7/9 rebuild programs. Unfortunately, on October 1, 1989, the rebuild programs ceased and the Shops were closed. A few units were rebuilt for the Mexican railroads in the early 1990's and Gunderson operates in a very small part of the shops, but the facility is largely abandoned today.

Besides the early 2-8-0 steam locomotives and CF7 rebuild programs, Cleburne Shops has been home to other programs as well. In 1970, the Shops released a locomotive that had an EMD 567-B prime mover rated at 1500 horsepower, a GP7 long hood, Blomberg trucks, but built on a Baldwin VO 1000 frame, utilizing the Baldwin cab. The unit was equipped with an EMD electrical cabinet. The control stand was also rebuilt and modeled after the GP7 stand which was also incorporated into the CF7 program. It was also equipped with the two-stack exhaust system which was employed on the first 36 CF7's. In order to build up the frame, a deck was created which was at a minimum of 4-inches thick, but in places was built up to 8 inches. One major problem was encountered -- how to create the center plates for the trucks. The men had to fabricate a design which allowed for the EMD trucks to be accepted by the Baldwin body. The unit was #1160, but was renumbered #1460 later and served as the Cleburne yard switcher. Many local railfans referred to the unit as a "BEEP," part Baldwin, part Geep. The men of the Shops remembered the unit was an experiment to determine the extent of the skills of the shop personnel.

This unit was originally assigned to Saginaw, Texas, as the yard switcher. The crews thoroughly enjoyed the unit because it was considered to have both ideal weight and extra power over a typical switcher. The engine was to be serviced in Cleburne on a regular basis, but the Saginaw crews seldom gave it up on time because they

enjoyed the unit so much and feared not having it returned. The 1996 roster still has the unit appearing as an active locomotive on the Santa Fe system.

From November 1972 through December 1981, 242 GP7 units were rebuilt in the Shops as well. An additional 56 GP9's were rebuilt from January 1978 through May 1980. Air conditioning was added, angled cabs installed and, if equipped with dynamic brakes, the brakes were removed and the blisters welded over.

Slugs were rebuilt or created in Cleburne as well as road units. One particular unit was a three-axle Alco unit which had been cut down. The unit had only three compartments in the low hood, two for truck blowers and the third compartment housed the electrical cabinet. Besides interior space for sanders, the remaining space under the short hood was for concrete which helped to add weight to assist the tractive effort.

Another version of slugs was represented in the rebuild of an F7B. The slug #123 (drone as the Santa Fe referred to the units), was built from the cabless F7B #272B on October 5, 1978. A particular feature of all Cleburne-built slugs was the placement of a snow plow on one end of the unit. It was speculated by previous publications that this particular slug was built from a CF7 because it employed the same I-beam fish-belly sill found on those units. This was not the case; rather, it was an application of employing the same technology of the CF7 on a slug.

Other slugs were rebuilt in Cleburne from GP7's, but not from the Santa Fe roster. The Santa Fe turned instead to the Union Pacific and forwarded competitive bids to Omaha, Nebraska, to obtain the units.

A second series of slugs, the 4600-series, were built in Cleburne, but were designed to work the San Bernardino yards. The first four units left Cleburne with an unusual identifying mark which clearly pointed to their location of assembly. A Texas-shaped steel plate, with Cleburne clearly marked, had been attached to the units. Only after an inspector noticed the creativity of the Cleburne shop personnel was the practice discontinued.

The next rebuild program centered on GP38's. Fifty-nine units were rebuilt between September 1984 through August 1985. The units were renumbered from the 3500 series to the 2300 series.

ABOVE: What do you call a half-Baldwin, half-Geep? A BEEP, of course! Photo collection of Allen R. Johnson.

BELOW: The Kalamazoo, Lake Shore & Chicago Railway was the first recipient of a Santa Fe rebuilt-GP7, the 2110. It was purchased from NRE and became KLS&C 85. It was painted in a brilliant scheme that reflected the wine grape-growing region that it served. The rebuilt GP7's were similar-looking to the CF7's, but featured longer short-hoods and narrower cabs. Notice the blanked-out dynamic brakes; none of the rebuilt GP7's kept their dynamics. Photographed at Paw Paw, Michigan, by Jaime F.M. Serensits.

The CF7 Locomotive

ABOVE: Santa Fe F7 #336L will one day become ATSF 2551, and eventually wind up as Indiana Rail Road #2551. Photo was taken in Spring of 1973, just 6 months before its rebirth as a CF7. Photo by C.H. Humphreys, collection Steve Hottle.

BELOW: The first two CF7's, Santa Fe 2649 and 2648 pose at the Cleburne shops in 1970. Both units featured open sill construction and ACI labels. The dynamic brakes on 2649 are unique to it, as are the number boards on the rear of the unit. Notice the different horn placements, as well -- the brakeman's side horn is moved toward the rear of 2649. Both units retained cab features from the F-units, including the round roof and side windows. Photo courtesy Eldon Whitworth.

After the EMD rebuild programs, the Cleburne Shops looked at a couple of GE rebuild projects. The Santa Fe wanted the units to be more fuel efficient when they left the shops, but on the other hand, the rebuild programs for the General Electric locomotives was much more expensive than had originally been thought. A couple of items ran the costs up over the EMD projects. The cab was designed to eliminate all sharp edges and the control stand was also very costly to incorporate in the GE design. The other feature which was costly, but very efficient, was the placement of the fire extinguisher inside the

short cab in a bracket recessed in the door. The Shops were also under different management since Mr. Cramer had retired in 1980. Some of the shop personnel felt costs could have been cut in order to make the program more cost efficient, and therefore, adding more jobs, or at the very least, saving jobs.

The last major rebuild program to be conducted at Cleburne centered on the SF30C locomotives which were rebuilt from U36C's from the 8700 series. The initial order was for 97 of the units to be rebuilt. The units were down-rated to 3100 horsepower and the electrical components

were upgraded to DASH-8 specifications. The class unit, #8700, was rebuilt differently in many aspects from previous Cleburne projects. First, the unit was put in red primer long before the unit was ever rebuilt. Then the prime mover was dismantled piece-by-piece while still attached to the frame, unlike the CF7 project where the prime mover was removed from the frame and rebuilt using a cradle. The prime mover was then reassembled as a whole unit and placed back on the frame. Even with the fact that both hoods and the cab were cut down to the frame, the piecemeal approach added greatly to the man-hours

BELOW: The "BEEP" #1460 is towing a fellow Cleburne rebuild, SF30C #9517. The strange combination of Baldwin and EMD has actually outlived the CF7 on the Santa Fe. The BEEP sported silver trucks, just like the other units shopped at Cleburne. Unit was well-maintained on the inside and the outside. The 9517 left Cleburne in the ill-fated SPSF (Shouldn't Paint So Fast) scheme, which was a result of merger talks between the Santa Fe and the Southern Pacific. Photo collection of Allen R. Johnson.

OPPOSITE TOP: The only SF30B unit ever built by Santa Fe, #7200 (ex-6332) poses at the Cleburne Shops on July 11, 1987, prior to its first test run. The large fuel tank could hold 4000 gallons of diesel. Eventually, it was stripped of the 700 extra horsepower, and the unit traded-in its 7200 class number for non-descript 6419.

OPPOSITE BOTTOM: SF30C Class unit #9500 displays its rebuilt squared-off nose near Brownwood, Texas, on the point of a freight. The SF30C was more successful than the SF30B program, with 70 units rebuilt before the project was scrapped. Both photos collection of Allen R. Johnson.

needed to complete the rebuild project.

With the SF30C units, the air plate was assembled upside-down and uprighted to slide in place under the cab floor. The short and long hoods were manufactured in the shop, in the same fashion as the hoods for the CF7's. The cab was completely rebuilt and was welded to the frame. It was thought by the shop personnel that this rigid cab caused the entire frame to be too stiff on the open track. The units were numbered in the 9500-series, but the program was canceled after 70 units were rebuilt. The remaining U36C's continued in service as they were.

In 1987, a solitary SF30B unit was rebuilt, with hopes of a possible rebuild program on U23B's. The unit was upgraded from 2300 to 3000 horsepower and became the #7200. It was equipped with a 4000 gallon fuel tank for long-haul service. It was later down-rated to 2300 horsepower and renumbered to 6419. The program never caught on, and two short years later, the Cleburne Shops were closed.

After Mr. Cramer's retirement, some of the shop personnel felt the Shop itself did not competitively bid on other projects. Many believe it was due to this lack of competitiveness that led to Santa Fe's decision to close the shops.

With the exception of the Coach Shop and the Roundhouse, the Shops were largely intact as of December 7, 1996,

when I visited Cleburne, Texas, for a Shop reunion. Approximately 150 men and family members attended this reunion. You could see, feel and witness the pride they had in their various crafts and the products they helped to produce for the Santa Fe Railroad. A few of the men appeared surprised when they found out how many CF7's were still operating, but most agreed that they were instructed by the Shop Superintendent to build a stock and sturdy locomotive. The men were simply happy to hear that they had accomplished what Mr. C. W. Cramer had requested. Mr. S. D. Rawlins stated, "Cramer worked you hard, you worked hard for him, but he was one of the fairest men I have known."

The Cast of Characters
(in order of their appearance)

2649

Rebuild Date	2/70
F-unit no.	262C
F-unit type	F7
Current owner	Anthracite Ry. Historical Soc.
Previous owners	Blue Mountain & Reading; trade-in to GE
Notes	Scrapped; parts made into 2 F3's; only CF7 built with dynamic brakes. Long hood from a GP7B. Originally painted in navy with white trim, later received Warbonnet. Never received a square cab.

2648

Rebuild Date	7/70
F-unit no.	203C
F-unit type	F3
Current owner	ISCX 111
Previous owners	WATCO 11
Notes	ISCX 111 Lettered "Seapac." Oldest surviving CF7.

2647

Rebuild Date	8/70
F-unit no.	210L
F-unit type	F7
Current owner	Pioneer Valley 2647
Previous owners	Pinsly

2646

Rebuild Date	9/70
F-unit no.	200C
F-unit type	F7
Current owner	Texas and Northern 995
Previous owners	NRE

2645

Rebuild Date	10/70
F-unit no.	217L
F-unit type	F7
Current owner	
Previous owners	Amtrak 599
Notes	Retired & sold

2644

Rebuild Date	11/70
F-unit no.	222C
F-unit type	F7
Current owner	Redmont 101
Previous owners	Chattooga & Chickamauga 101; Columbus & Greenville 809; NRE

2643

Rebuild Date	1/71
F-unit no.	270L
F-unit type	F7
Current owner	Florida Midland 64
Previous owners	Florida Central 2643

2642

Rebuild Date	2/71
F-unit no.	27L
F-unit type	F3
Current owner	Econo-Rail 2642
Previous owners	

ABOVE: Ex-Santa Fe #2635, now Mississippi & Skuna Valley D-5, poses at Bruce, Mississippi, on October 26, 1987. The railroad is owned by the Weyerhaeuser Company and currently hauls mainly lumber. Photo by Jim Shaw.

OPPOSITE TOP: Watco #11 sits at a Hoechst-Celanese plant in Texas. Unit is former Santa Fe 2648. Compare this picture with photo of 2648 on page 45 when the unit was first released from Cleburne. It has a new cab, new horns, an orange beacon, a ground plane, a boxed frame and silver trucks. It also has a new pair of unusual spark arrestors. Photo by Cary F. Poole.

OPPOSITE BOTTOM: Santa Cruz, Big Trees and Pacific 2641 rolls Chrough Santa Cruz on June 29, 1996. The 2641 also traded-in its round cab for an angled cab. It appears that its two stacks are covered with wire mesh to keep sparking to a minimum. Note extra-long front window for the engineer. Photo by Evan Werkema.

ABOVE: Keokuk Junction temporarily leased the 2632 in 1994. The unit had formerly seen service on the Quad Cities Rocket Dinner Train. Note the faint "Quad Cities" lettering on the long hood, just ahead of the word "Rocket". Also note stenciling on frame reading "2632 QCRD". Unit was dubbed "The Rocket" while on the KJRY. The rear side cab window is plated over and the engineer has the original small window in front. The 2632 is owned by NRE. Photo taken February 24, 1994, in Keokuk, Iowa, by Jeffrey Dobek.

BELOW: Zacky Farms' bright CF7 is former Santa Fe 2631, the nineteenth CF7 turned loose from Cleburne. Although it retains its two-stack configuration, it has traded traded its round roof for an angular cab. Quonset-hut-shaped contraption on cab roof is an anti-theft device for the horn. This Zacky CF7 is one of several "Chicken Switchers" along Route 99 in California, so-called for their service to feed mills. Photographed by Kel Aiken on April 10, 1995, at Travers, California.

ABOVE: A pair of CF7's leading a pair of six-axle units on a hot intermodal train??? It really happened at Emporia, Kansas, in late Fall of 1984. The lead CF7 had a round cab and two exhausts, no less! I wonder what the crews were thinking this day? Believe it or not, unit was retired about a month later; from star to the scrapline in only 30 days. Photographed by C.H. Humphreys, collection of Steve Hottle.

BELOW: The 2615 was traded-in to General Electric and was sold in-turn to Mid-Texas International, where it was renumbered to 1002. Although painted in an interesting scheme, this pair has never been known to be used in revenue service or lettered since leaving the Santa Fe. Photographed on December 28, 1985, at MKT's Ray Yard in Denison, Texas, by Jimmy Barlow.

BELOW: Round-roofed Maryland and Delaware #2628 is seen at Selbyville, Maryland on May 16, 1991. The MDDE has another CF7, ex-Santa Fe 2531, which was renumbered to 2630. Photo by Jim Shaw.

OPPOSITE: The Louisiana & Delta #1501, named "City of New Iberia", is on a siding in New Iberia, Louisiana, waiting for a Southern Pacific freight to pass on August 3, 1991. Photo by Cary F. Poole.

2641

Rebuild Date	3/71
F-unit no.	222L
F-unit type	F7
Current owner	Santa Cruz, Big Trees & Pacific 2641
Previous owners	

2640

Rebuild Date	3/71
F-unit no.	310L
F-unit type	F7
Current owner	Delta Southern 107
Previous owners	NRE

2639

Rebuild Date	4/71
F-unit no.	44C
F-unit type	F7
Current owner	Scrapped
Previous owners	
Notes	Southwest Railway Car Parts

2638

Rebuild Date	5/71
F-unit no.	204C
F-unit type	F7
Current owner	Scrapped
Previous owners	
Notes	Naporano Iron & Metal

2637

Rebuild Date	7/71
F-unit no.	246C
F-unit type	F7
Current owner	Florida Midland 2637
Previous owners	Florida Central 2637

2636

Rebuild Date	8/71
F-unit no.	31C
F-unit type	F3
Current owner	BNSF 402
Previous owners	Washington Central 402; NRE

2635

Rebuild Date	9/71
F-unit no.	40C
F-unit type	F7
Current owner	Mississippi & Skuna Valley D-5
Previous owners	NRE; trade-in to GE

2634

Rebuild Date	10/71
F-unit no.	43L
F-unit type	F7
Current owner	Scrapped
Previous owners	
Notes	Commercial Metals (wrecked @ Peabody, Kansas, 7/76)

2633

Rebuild Date	11/71
F-unit no.	312L
F-unit type	F7
Current owner	WATCO 6
Previous owners	

2632

Rebuild Date	12/71
F-unit no.	47L
F-unit type	F7
Current owner	NRE 2632
Previous owners	BM&R; trade-in to GE
Notes	Previously leased to Keokuk Junction; Quad City Rocket

2631

Rebuild Date	12/71
F-unit no.	313C (34C)
F-unit type	F7
Current owner	Zacky Farms 2631
Previous owners	Econo-Rail 2631
Notes	Remote controlled

2630

Rebuild Date	1/72
F-unit no.	18C
F-unit type	F3
Current owner	Scrapped
Previous owners	
Notes	Metal Processing Industries (wrecked @ Zephyr, TX, 3/80)

2629

Rebuild Date	2/72
F-unit no.	20L
F-unit type	F3
Current owner	Delta Southern 105
Previous owners	NRE

2628

Rebuild Date	3/72
F-unit no.	20C
F-unit type	F3
Current owner	Maryland & Delaware 2628
Previous owners	NRE; Blue Mountain & Reading; trade-in to GE

2627

Rebuild Date	3/72
F-unit no.	21L
F-unit type	F3
Current owner	Midwest Coal Handling 2627
Previous owners	

2626

Rebuild Date	3/72
F-unit no.	22C
F-unit type	F3
Current owner	Delta Southern 102
Previous owners	National Railway Equipment

2625

Rebuild Date	4/72
F-unit no.	24C
F-unit type	F3
Current owner	Scrapped
Previous owners	
Notes	Cut-up by Southwest Railway Car Parts

2624

Rebuild Date	4/72
F-unit no.	35C
F-unit type	F3
Current owner	Econo-Rail 2624
Previous owners	

2623

Rebuild Date	4/72
F-unit no.	24L
F-unit type	F3
Current owner	Rescar 2623
Previous owners	

2622

Rebuild Date	5/72
F-unit no.	19L
F-unit type	F3
Current owner	Louisiana & Delta 1501
Previous owners	
Notes	Unit is named "City of New Iberia"

2621

Rebuild Date	5/72
F-unit no.	227L
F-unit type	F7
Current owner	Louisiana & Delta 7003
Previous owners	KCS; MidSouth 7003; National Railway Equipment

ABOVE: Boise Cascade's Wallula, Washington, plant provides an impressive background for WATX 6, and notice how clean unit and facility are kept. WATCO has a contract to switch this facility. The #6 was former Santa Fe 2633, the 17th CF7 built. Unit retains its original two-exhaust system and its Santa Fe number boards, but no longer has a round cab. Note that the classification lights have been painted over. Photographed August 10, 1994, by Kel Aiken.

BELOW: This pair of Delta Southern CF7's is spotted at McGehee, Arkansas, on November 20, 1995. The Delta Southern operates a roster full of CF7's and is owned by NRE. Despite being relatively early rebuilds (2605 and 2585) they both now have four stacks and angled cabs. Photo by Kel Aiken.

The CF7 Locomotive

ABOVE: Aberdeen & Rockfish operated this attractively-painted CF7 until a grade crossing accident put it out of commission in 1996. Notice unique track arrangement in foreground -- 3-way stub switch -- very rare! Photo by Cary F. Poole.

BELOW: Midsouth 7005 at Artesia, Mississippi, during late summer of 1990. Remarkably, this is the same locomotive that is pictured on page 41, former Santa Fe #2591. Unit now has square cab and a new set of horns. The 7005 also has an elongated front window for the engineer. After purchase by the KCS and subsequent repurchase by Genesee & Wyoming, unit will become Louisiana & Delta 1509. Photo by Tom Sink.

2620

Rebuild Date	5/72
F-unit no.	202C
F-unit type	F7
Current owner	Scrapped
Previous owners	
Notes	Metal Processing Industries

2619

Rebuild Date	5/72
F-unit no.	201C
F-unit type	F3
Current owner	Los Angeles Junction 2619
Previous owners	

2618

Rebuild Date	6/72
F-unit no.	27C
F-unit type	F3
Current owner	Louisiana & Delta 1500
Previous owners	NRE
Notes	Currently named "Port of Lake Charles"; was previously named "Patoutville"

2617

Rebuild Date	6/72
F-unit no.	31L
F-unit type	F3
Current owner	Indiana Rail Road 2617
Previous owners	
Notes	For parts

2616

Rebuild Date	6/72
F-unit no.	16C
F-unit type	F3
Current owner	Rail Switching Services 1802
Previous owners	KCS; MidSouth 7011; MidSouth 7004:1; NRE
Notes	Currently leased to Union Camp Paper Mill

2615

Rebuild Date	6/72
F-unit no.	19C
F-unit type	F3
Current owner	Mid Texas International 1002
Previous owners	trade-in to GE

2614

Rebuild Date	7/72
F-unit no.	33L
F-unit type	F3
Current owner	Red River Valley & Western 309
Previous owners	NRE

2613

Rebuild Date	7/72
F-unit no.	23L
F-unit type	F3
Current owner	Scrapped
Previous owners	
Notes	Southwest Railway Car Parts

2612

Rebuild Date	7/72
F-unit no.	272L
F-unit type	F7
Current owner	Gloster Southern 1502
Previous owners	
Notes	Rebuilt by AD&N 6/86

2611

Rebuild Date	8/72
F-unit no.	251L
F-unit type	F7
Current owner	Scrapped
Previous owners	
Notes	Metal Processing Industries

2610

Rebuild Date	8/72
F-unit no.	228C
F-unit type	F7
Current owner	Scrapped
Previous owners	
Notes	Southwest Railway Car Parts

2609

Rebuild Date	8/72
F-unit no.	29L
F-unit type	F3
Current owner	Louisiana & Delta 1507
Previous owners	KCS; MidSouth 7002:2; NRE
Notes	named "Breaux Bridge"

2608

Rebuild Date	8/72
F-unit no.	211L
F-unit type	F7
Current owner	Econo-rail 2608
Previous owners	
Notes	Worked at Kraft Foods, was also seen dead-in-transit; Lettered "Baytank"

2607

Rebuild Date	8/72
F-unit no.	274L
F-unit type	F7
Current owner	Delta Southern 106
Previous owners	NRE

2606

Rebuild Date	8/72
F-unit no.	220C
F-unit type	F7
Current owner	WATCO 7
Previous owners	

2605

Rebuild Date	9/72
F-unit no.	260L
F-unit type	F7
Current owner	Delta Southern 104
Previous owners	NRE

2604

Rebuild Date	9/72
F-unit no.	278L
F-unit type	F7
Current owner	Econo-Rail 2604
Previous owners	

2603

Rebuild Date	9/72
F-unit no.	265L
F-unit type	F7
Current owner	Allegheny 113
Previous owners	Blue Mountain & Reading; trade-in to GE
Notes	For parts

2602

Rebuild Date	9/72
F-unit no.	234C
F-unit type	F7
Current owner	Econo-Rail 2602
Previous owners	

2601

Rebuild Date	10/72
F-unit no.	214L
F-unit type	F7
Current owner	Scrapped
Previous owners	
Notes	Scrapped locally in Los Angeles

2600

Rebuild Date	10/72
F-unit no.	248L
F-unit type	F7
Current owner	Santa Cruz, Big Trees & Pacific
Previous owners	

2599

Rebuild Date	10/72
F-unit no.	266L
F-unit type	F7
Current owner	Scrapped
Previous owners	
Notes	Southwest Railway Car Parts

2598

Rebuild Date	10/72
F-unit no.	254L
F-unit type	F7
Current owner	Corn Products Corp. 2598
Previous owners	Mountain Diesel Transportation

2597

Rebuild Date	10/72
F-unit no.	247C
F-unit type	F7
Current owner	Pioneer Valley 2597
Previous owners	trade-in to GE
Notes	Went first to Frankfort & Cincinnati, another Pinsly property

2596

Rebuild Date	11/72
F-unit no.	212C
F-unit type	F7
Current owner	NRE
Previous owners	KCS 7015; MidSouth 7015; NRE

2595

Rebuild Date	11/72
F-unit no.	211C
F-unit type	F7
Current owner	
Previous owners	Amtrak 598
Notes	Retired & sold

2594

Rebuild Date	11/72
F-unit no.	209C
F-unit type	F7
Current owner	Aberdeen & Rockfish 2594
Previous owners	Blue Mountain & Reading; trade-in to GE
Notes	Wrecked & totaled

BELOW: Sierra had their CF7 #594 for only a short time. This ex-Amtrak unit was obtained from Nevada Industrial Switching, then returned. Photographed at Oakdale, California, on June 24, 1995, by Evan Werkema.

2593

Rebuild Date	11/72
F-unit no.	214C
F-unit type	F7
Current owner	Econo-Rail 2593
Previous owners	
Notes	Works at Port of Beaumont

2592

Rebuild Date	11/72
F-unit no.	231C
F-unit type	F7
Current owner	
Previous owners	Amtrak 597
Notes	Retired & sold

2591

Rebuild Date	12/72
F-unit no.	235L
F-unit type	F7
Current owner	Louisiana & Delta 7005
Previous owners	KCS; MidSouth 7005; NRE

2590

Rebuild Date	12/72
F-unit no.	269L
F-unit type	F7
Current owner	Louisiana & Delta 303
Previous owners	Allegheny & Eastern 303; Allegheny 103; Blue Mountain & Reading

2589

Rebuild Date	12/72
F-unit no.	243L
F-unit type	F7
Current owner	G&W Switching Services 1514
Previous owners	KCS; MidSouth 7014; NRE

2588

Rebuild Date	12/72
F-unit no.	273C
F-unit type	F7
Current owner	
Previous owners	Amtrak 596
Notes	Retired & sold

2587

Rebuild Date	1/73
F-unit no.	241C (205L)
F-unit type	F7
Current owner	Naporano Iron & Metal 595
Previous owners	Amtrak 595

2586

Rebuild Date	1/73
F-unit no.	244C
F-unit type	F7
Current owner	G&W Switching Services 1510
Previous owners	KCS; MidSouth 7006; NRE

2585

Rebuild Date	1/73
F-unit no.	264C
F-unit type	F7
Current owner	Delta Southern 100
Previous owners	NRE

2584

Rebuild Date	1/73
F-unit no.	277C
F-unit type	F7
Current owner	Nevada Industrial Switching 594
Previous owners	Sierra 594; Nevada Industrial Switching 594; Amtrak 594

2583

Rebuild Date	2/73
F-unit no.	249L
F-unit type	F7
Current owner	Scrapped
Previous owners	
Notes	Wrecked at Los Angeles 3/84

2582

Rebuild Date	2/73
F-unit no.	250C
F-unit type	F7
Current owner	Econo-Rail 2582
Previous owners	

ABOVE: Washington Central "Hooter" number 401 switches refrigerated cars ar Prosser, Washington, in August 1991, on the former Northern Pacific mainline. Note odd placement of horns on the top of the long hood, near the rear of the unit. This unit is now owned by BNSF and stored dead at Interbay, Washington. Photo by Gary D. Munsey, Sr.

BELOW: Tennessee Southern 201 ducks under a highway overpass near Columbia, Tennessee, on October 25, 1995. The TS 201 was formerly Indiana Rail Rail Road 201, and originally Santa Fe 2539. Notice gold numbers painted on rear of unit where number boards would be. Unit is a four-stacker with a low-profile antenna mounted on its ground plate. Photo by Kel Aiken.

LEFT: RESCAR 2535 and 2507 are assigned to switch the enormous White Crust Flour Co. (proud sponsors of the White Crust Flour "Dough Boys") elevator at Saginaw, Texas. Photo taken Spring, 1991, by Cary F. Poole.

BELOW: Hollis and Eastern 2520 is the biggest power on this small railroad in Oklahoma. Although completely repainted, the old frame markings from the Santa Fe were carefully touched up, including the "Cleburne" designation. This handsome unit has the extra-length engineer's window and the white pilot shows excellent detail; you can easily spot the anti-climber and buffer plate remaining from its previous life as an F-unit. Photo by Cary F. Poole.

BELOW: Red River Valley & Western number 304 poses at Carrington, North Dakota, in late Spring of 1988. The RRV&W originally had a fleet of 10 CF7's, numbered 300-309. They have since sold the 300 and 306 to South Dakota Wheat Growers. They are in the process of converting number 303 to a slug at a facility on the Twin Cities & Western (their sister railroad), where it may stay, and are planning to convert 302 and 305 to slugs in the future. Photo by Tom Sink.

ABOVE: Los Angeles Junction Railway CF7 #2563 is ex-228L. It is seen here in Los Angeles on January 24, 1987. Photo by Brian Griebenow, collection of Gordon C. Bassett.

2581

Rebuild Date	2/73
F-unit no.	267L
F-unit type	F7
Current owner	Econo-Rail 2581
Previous owners	

2580

Rebuild Date	2/73
F-unit no.	276C
F-unit type	F7
Current owner	Econo-Rail 2580
Previous owners	

2579

Rebuild Date	3/73
F-unit no.	221L
F-unit type	F7
Current owner	Econo-Rail 2579
Previous owners	
Notes	Works at DuPont

2578

Rebuild Date	4/73
F-unit no.	230L
F-unit type	F7
Current owner	BNSF 401
Previous owners	Washington Central 401; NRE

2577

Rebuild Date	4/73
F-unit no.	204L
F-unit type	F7
Current owner	G&W Switching Services 1512
Previous owners	KCS; MidSouth 7008; NRE
Notes	Named "Bill Sjolander Yard"

2576

Rebuild Date	4/73
F-unit no.	223L
F-unit type	F7
Current owner	Mid Texas International 1001
Previous owners	trade-in to GE

2575

Rebuild Date	4/73
F-unit no.	233L
F-unit type	F7
Current owner	Econo-Rail 2575
Previous owners	

2574

Rebuild Date	4/73
F-unit no.	271L
F-unit type	F7
Current owner	Silcott
Previous owners	DuPont 2574; NRE; Blue Mountain & Reading; trade-in to GE

2573

Rebuild Date	5/73
F-unit no.	248C
F-unit type	F7
Current owner	Rail Switching Services 1801
Previous owners	KCS; MidSouth 7009; NRE
Notes	Currently leased to Union Camp Paper Mill

2572

Rebuild Date	5/73
F-unit no.	206L
F-unit type	F7
Current owner	Econo-Rail 2572
Previous owners	

2571

Rebuild Date	5/73
F-unit no.	202L
F-unit type	F7
Current owner	Los Angeles Junction 2571
Previous owners	

2570

Rebuild Date	5/73
F-unit no.	242C
F-unit type	F7
Current owner	Delta Southern 101
Previous owners	NRE

2569

Rebuild Date	5/73
F-unit no.	213C
F-unit type	F7
Current owner	Econo-Rail 2569
Previous owners	
Notes	Was leased to Fort Worth & Western 2569

2568

Rebuild Date	6/73
F-unit no.	226L
F-unit type	F7
Current owner	Los Angeles Junction 2568
Previous owners	

2567

Rebuild Date	6/73
F-unit no.	244L
F-unit type	F7
Current owner	Scrapped
Previous owners	
Notes	Southwest Railway Car Parts

2566

Rebuild Date	6/73
F-unit no.	216C
F-unit type	F7
Current owner	G&W Switching Services 1513
Previous owners	KCS; MidSouth 7013; National Railway Equipment

2565

Rebuild Date	6/73
F-unit no.	302C (34L)
F-unit type	F3
Current owner	Pioneer Valley 2565
Previous owners	Pinsly

2564

Rebuild Date	7/73
F-unit no.	305C (38C)
F-unit type	F7
Current owner	Columbus & Greenville
Previous owners	KCS; MidSouth 7004:2; NRE
	Bought for parts, still lettered MidSouth

2563

Rebuild Date	7/73
F-unit no.	228L
F-unit type	F7
Current owner	Los Angeles Junction 2563
Previous owners	

2562

Rebuild Date	7/73
F-unit no.	280C
F-unit type	F7
Current owner	Sierra 593
Previous owners	Nevada Industrial Switching 593; Amtrak 593

2561

Rebuild Date	7/73
F-unit no.	230C
F-unit type	F7
Current owner	NRE
Previous owners	KCS 7010; MidSouth 7010; National Railway Equipment

2560

Rebuild Date	7/73
F-unit no.	240C
F-unit type	F7
Current owner	Econo-Rail 2560
Previous owners	

2559

Rebuild Date	8/73
F-unit no.	303C (47C)
F-unit type	F7
Current owner	Rail Link 559
Previous owners	Nashville & Eastern 2559; Tennken

2558

Rebuild Date	8/73
F-unit no.	311C (45L)
F-unit type	F7
Current owner	Pioneer Valley 2558
Previous owners	trade-in to GE
Notes	Went first to Frankfort & Cincinnati (Pinsly)

2557

Rebuild Date	8/73
F-unit no.	302L
F-unit type	F7
Current owner	Scrapped
Previous owners	
Notes	Commercial Metals

2556

Rebuild Date	8/73
F-unit no.	309C (23C)
F-unit type	F3
Current owner	Scrapped
Previous owners	
Notes	Metal Processing Industries (wrecked Meridian, TX, 8/79)

2555

Rebuild Date	8/73
F-unit no.	207L
F-unit type	F7
Current owner	Rail Link 555
Previous owners	West Tennessee; Nashville & Eastern 2555; Tennken

2554

Rebuild Date	9/73
F-unit no.	308C (22L)
F-unit type	F3
Current owner	Metal Processing Industries
Previous owners	Los Angeles Junction
Notes	Scrapped

2553

Rebuild Date	9/73
F-unit no.	257C
F-unit type	F7
Current owner	Rail Link 553
Previous owners	Nashville & Eastern 2553; Tennken

2552

Rebuild Date	9/73
F-unit no.	243C
F-unit type	F7
Current owner	Scrapped
Previous owners	

2551

Rebuild Date	9/73
F-unit no.	336L
F-unit type	F7
Current owner	
Previous owners	Indiana Rail Road 2551
Notes	Sold or scrapped

2550

Rebuild Date	10/73
F-unit no.	278C
F-unit type	F7
Current owner	Texas and Northern 994
Previous owners	NRE

2549

Rebuild Date	10/73
F-unit no.	208C
F-unit type	F7
Current owner	WATCO 1002
Previous owners	South East Kansas 1002; WATCO 1002

2548

Rebuild Date	10/73
F-unit no.	257L
F-unit type	F7
Current owner	Columbus & Greenville 806
Previous owners	NRE

2547

Rebuild Date	10/73
F-unit no.	231L
F-unit type	F7
Current owner	Rail Link 547
Previous owners	Nashville & Eastern 2547; Tennken

2546

Rebuild Date	11/73
F-unit no.	229L
F-unit type	F7
Current owner	Kentucky Ry. Museum 2546
Previous owners	Indiana Rail Road 2546
Notes	Never repainted; only preserved CF7

2545

Rebuild Date	11/73
F-unit no.	256C
F-unit type	F7
Current owner	Econo-Rail 2545
Previous owners	
Notes	Scrapped for spare parts

2544

Rebuild Date	11/73
F-unit no.	249C
F-unit type	F7
Current owner	Dodge City Ford & Bucklin 1001
Previous owners	South East Kansas 1001; WATCO

2543

Rebuild Date	11/73
F-unit no.	300C (46C)
F-unit type	F7
Current owner	Indiana Rail Road 2543
Previous owners	

2542

Rebuild Date	11/73
F-unit no.	218C
F-unit type	F7
Current owner	Osage 1000
Previous owners	South East Kansas 1000; WATCO

2541

Rebuild Date	12/73
F-unit no.	240L
F-unit type	F7
Current owner	Econo-Rail 2541
Previous owners	
Notes	Scrapped for spare parts

ABOVE: Texas & Northern #992 is a long way from home, having been photographed in late Spring of 1989 in Asheville, North Carolina (note how neatly the four stacks are capped), on its way to Great Smoky Mountains Railway, where it would be leased for the next three years. The 992 is former Santa Fe 2501. Photo by Tom Sink.

ABOVE: After arriving on Great Smoky Mountains Railway property, number 992 received a bright paint scheme and was assigned to passenger service. Photo by Tom Sink.

RIGHT: Following three years of excursion service, it was back to the Texas industrial scene. The GSMR oval was filled in and a stylized "TN" was added. "Texas & Northern" was spelled along the long hood, and it was time for 992 to get back to work. The rigors of heavy industrial switching had taken its toll on the 992, as illustrated by this photo in Lone Star, Texas, on November 19, 1992; it had lost part of its pilot, its warning beacon, and was covered in oil. Photo by Kel Aiken.

LEFT: Iowa Northern's 2493 looks radiant in this beautiful yellow scheme, as it rests at Waterloo, Iowa, in late summer of 1989. Unit has four stacks and the ground plate sits behind the air conditioner. The 2493 has since been sold and is used by Arkansas Midland, a member of the Pinsly family of railroads. Photograph by Tom Sink.

RIGHT: This smart-looking CF7 is operated by AT&L, and this is not the first time that it wore a green paint scheme! The unit was previously the Harvester CF7 (see page 100). This is AT&L's only CF7. Photo taken November 24, 1995, in Calumet, Oklahoma, by Kel Aiken.

LEFT: Keokuk Junction 488 at Keokuk Junction, Iowa, on December 8, 1992. Note number on side of nose, rather than side of cab, reminiscent of the DT&I. For a short time, the KJRY operated two CF7's, the other being the former Quad Cities Rocket Dinner Train 2632 on lease from NRE (see page 50). Currently, this is the only CF7 they own, and the only one to wear KJRY's nifty orange scheme. This unit previously operated in plain grey. Jeffrey Dobek photo.

2540

Rebuild Date	12/73
F-unit no.	219C
F-unit type	F7
Current owner	Scrapped
Previous owners	
Notes	Metal Processing Industries

2539

Rebuild Date	12/73
F-unit no.	221C
F-unit type	F7
Current owner	Tennessee Southern 201
Previous owners	Indiana Rail Road 201

2538

Rebuild Date	1/74
F-unit no.	307L
F-unit type	F7
Current owner	NRE
Previous owners	KCS 7012; MidSouth 7012; MidSouth 7002:2; NRE

2537

Rebuild Date	1/74
F-unit no.	233C
F-unit type	F7
Current owner	Econo-Rail 2537
Previous owners	
Notes	Scrapped for spare parts

2536

Rebuild Date	1/74
F-unit no.	242L
F-unit type	F7
Current owner	Rail Link 536
Previous owners	Nashville & Eastern 2536; Tennken

2535

Rebuild Date	2/74
F-unit no.	304C (38L)
F-unit type	F7
Current owner	RESCAR 2535
Previous owners	

2534

Rebuild Date	2/74
F-unit no.	309L
F-unit type	F7
Current owner	Econo-Rail 2534
Previous owners	

2533

Rebuild Date	2/74
F-unit no.	255L
F-unit type	F7
Current owner	Inman Service 5
Previous owners	WATCO 5
Notes	Will later be r# to WATCO 5; Previously leased to Asarco

2532

Rebuild Date	2/74
F-unit no.	266C
F-unit type	F7
Current owner	
Previous owners	Indiana Rail Road 2532
Notes	Sold or scrapped

2531

Rebuild Date	3/74
F-unit no.	310C (42C)
F-unit type	F7
Current owner	Maryland & Delaware 2630
Previous owners	NRE; Blue Mountain & Reading; trade-in to GE

2530

Rebuild Date	3/74
F-unit no.	209L
F-unit type	F7
Current owner	Texas and Northern 993
Previous owners	Leased to Great Smoky Mountain 993 for three years; Texas and Northern 993; NRE

2529

Rebuild Date	3/74
F-unit no.	276L
F-unit type	F7
Current owner	Rail Link 529
Previous owners	Nashville & Eastern 2529; Tennken

2528

Rebuild Date	3/74
F-unit no.	239L
F-unit type	F7
Current owner	
Previous owners	Indiana Rail Road 2528
Notes	Sold or scrapped

2527

Rebuild Date	3/74
F-unit no.	327L (308L)
F-unit type	F7
Current owner	
Previous owners	Indiana Rail Road 200
Notes	Sold or scrapped

2526

Rebuild Date	4/74
F-unit no.	251C
F-unit type	F7
Current owner	Econo-Rail 2526
Previous owners	

2525

Rebuild Date	4/74
F-unit no.	344L
F-unit type	F7
Current owner	Midwest Coal Handling 2525
Previous owners	Nashville & Eastern 2525; Tennken

2524

Rebuild Date	4/74
F-unit no.	216L
F-unit type	F7
Current owner	Red River Valley & Western 305
Previous owners	NRE; trade-in to GE

2523

Rebuild Date	4/74
F-unit no.	277L
F-unit type	F7
Current owner	Rail Link 523
Previous owners	Nashville & Eastern 2523; Tennken

2522

Rebuild Date	5/74
F-unit no.	255C
F-unit type	F7
Current owner	Arkansas, Louisiana & Mississippi 1514
Previous owners	Ashley Drew & Northern 1514

2521

Rebuild Date	5/74
F-unit no.	264L
F-unit type	F7
Current owner	Louisiana & Delta 304
Previous owners	Allegheny & Eastern 304; Allegheny 104; Allegheny 111; Blue Mountain & Reading; trade-in to GE

2520

Rebuild Date	5/74
F-unit no.	282C
F-unit type	F9
Current owner	Hollis & Eastern 2520
Previous owners	RESCAR

2519

Rebuild Date	5/74
F-unit no.	289L
F-unit type	F9
Current owner	Scrapped
Previous owners	
Notes	Southwest Railway Car Parts

2518

Rebuild Date	6/74
F-unit no.	312C (36C)
F-unit type	F3
Current owner	Rail Link 518
Previous owners	Nashville & Eastern 2518; Tennken 2518

2517

Rebuild Date	6/74
F-unit no.	315L
F-unit type	F7
Current owner	Rail Link 517
Previous owners	Commonwealth 517; Nashville & Eastern 2517; Tennken

2516

Rebuild Date	6/74
F-unit no.	272C
F-unit type	F7
Current owner	Econo-Rail 2516
Previous owners	

2515

Rebuild Date	7/74
F-unit no.	287L
F-unit type	F9
Current owner	Indiana Rail Road 2515
Previous owners	
Notes	For parts

2514

Rebuild Date	7/74
F-unit no.	279L
F-unit type	F7
Current owner	Red River Valley & Western 304
Previous owners	NRE; trade-in to GE

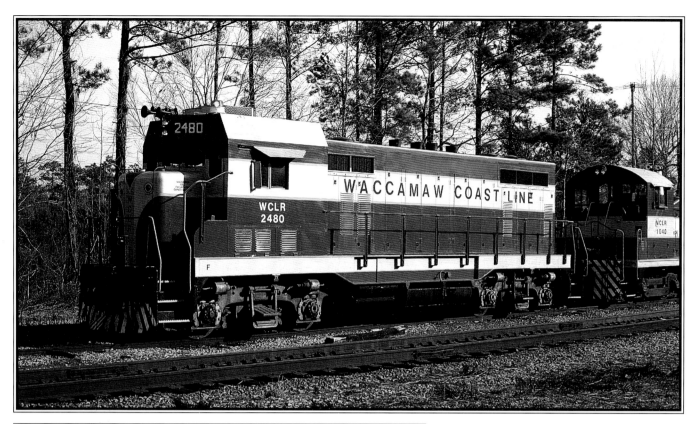

ABOVE: The Waccamaw Coast Line operated this CF7 in a resplendent purple and silver scheme, similar to that worn by cab units of the Atlantic Coast Line. The unit looks very similar today, except for Clinton Terminal lettering and reporting marks in place of Waccamaw Coast Line's. Photographed at Conway, South Carolina, late in 1989, by Tom Sink.

LEFT: Fort Worth and Western's colorful CF7 features "Cahoots" the Tarantula displayed prominently on the nose. Notice the new piece bolted on the bottom of the pilot and the conspicuous spark arrestors. Photographed at Northeast 23rd Street, on Fort Worth's north side, near the stockyards on September 24, 1993, by Wes Carr.

RIGHT: IMC 204 rests in its Port Tampa, Florida, home in January 1990. Notice that the main cab window sits far to the front of the cab, and there is an extra side cab window. Note also the small second window in front for the engineer. Photo by Tom Sink.

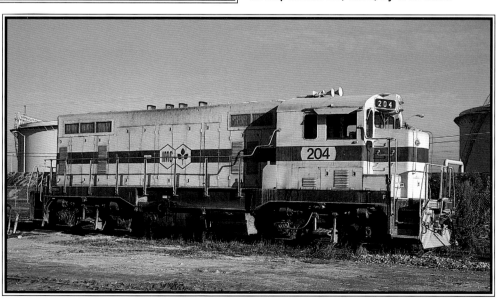

2513

Rebuild Date	7/74
F-unit no.	218L
F-unit type	F7
Current owner	
Previous owners	Amtrak 592
Notes	Retired & sold

2512

Rebuild Date	7/74
F-unit no.	304L
F-unit type	F7
Current owner	Commonwealth 512
Previous owners	Nashville & Eastern 2512; Tennken

2511

Rebuild Date	7/74
F-unit no.	232L
F-unit type	F7
Current owner	Illinois Railway Supply
Previous owners	Midwest Coal Handling 2511
Notes	Scrapped

2510

Rebuild Date	7/74
F-unit no.	217C
F-unit type	F7
Current owner	Econo-Rail 2510
Previous owners	
Notes	Scrapped, used for spare parts

2509

Rebuild Date	8/74
F-unit no.	224L
F-unit type	F7
Current owner	Florida Northern 50
Previous owners	Cadillac & Lake City 50; Railroad Inc

2508

Rebuild Date	8/74
F-unit no.	314L
F-unit type	F7
Current owner	Midwest Coal Handling 2508
Previous owners	

2507

Rebuild Date	8/74
F-unit no.	313L
F-unit type	F7
Current owner	RESCAR 2507
Previous owners	

2506

Rebuild Date	8/74
F-unit no.	203L
F-unit type	F7
Current owner	Tennessee Southern 2506
Previous owners	Indiana Rail Road 2506

2505

Rebuild Date	8/74
F-unit no.	239C
F-unit type	F7
Current owner	Columbus & Greenville 807
Previous owners	NRE

2504

Rebuild Date	8/74
F-unit no.	284C
F-unit type	F9
Current owner	G&W Switching Services 1511
Previous owners	KCS; MidSouth 7007; NRE

2503

Rebuild Date	9/74
F-unit no.	268C
F-unit type	F7
Current owner	Florida Central 53
Previous owners	
Notes	Was last CF7 on ATSF roster

2502

Rebuild Date	9/74
F-unit no.	280L
F-unit type	F7
Current owner	Scrapped
Previous owners	
Notes	Valley Steel & Supply (wrecked @ San Bernardino, CA, 7/79)

2501

Rebuild Date	9/74
F-unit no.	262L
F-unit type	F7
Current owner	Texas and Northern 992
Previous owners	Leased to Great Smoky Mountain 992 for three years; Texas and Northern 992; NRE

2500

Rebuild Date	9/74
F-unit no.	343L
F-unit type	F7
Current owner	Juliana Coal 2500
Previous owners	Blue Mountain & Reading; trade-in to GE

2499

Rebuild Date	10/74
F-unit no.	256L
F-unit type	F7
Current owner	Red River Valley & Western 303
Previous owners	NRE; trade-in to GE

2498

Rebuild Date	10/74
F-unit no.	303L
F-unit type	F7
Current owner	Scrapped
Previous owners	
Notes	Southwest Railway Car Parts

2497

Rebuild Date	10/74
F-unit no.	253L
F-unit type	F7
Current owner	
Previous owners	
Notes	Scrapped

2496

Rebuild Date	10/74
F-unit no.	253C
F-unit type	F7
Current owner	DuPont Chemicals 7001
Previous owners	ADM; Eastern Illinois 7001; KCS; MidSouth 7001; NRE

2495

Rebuild Date	10/74
F-unit no.	310L (44L)
F-unit type	F7
Current owner	Midwest Coal Handling 2495
Previous owners	

2494

Rebuild Date	11/74
F-unit no.	311L
F-unit type	F7
Current owner	Florida Central 49
Previous owners	Florida Central 2494; Railroad Inc.
Notes	On Greenville & Northern (Pinsly) several months 1995 while their locomotive was being repaired.

2493

Rebuild Date	2493
F-unit no.	300L
F-unit type	F7
Current owner	Arkansas Midland 2493
Previous owners	Iowa Northern 2493
Notes	Plan to renumber to 493 later

2492

Rebuild Date	11/74
F-unit no.	301L
F-unit type	F7
Current owner	Midwest Coal Handling 2492
Previous owners	
Notes	For parts

2491

Rebuild Date	12/74
F-unit no.	312L (37C)
F-unit type	F7
Current owner	AT&L 2491
Previous owners	Harvesters Grain 2491; NRE; Railroad Inc.

2490

Rebuild Date	12/74
F-unit no.	314C (32C)
F-unit type	F3
Current owner	Arkansas, Louisiana & Mississippi 1513
Previous owners	Ashley, Drew & Northern 1513

2489

Rebuild Date	12/74
F-unit no.	206C
F-unit type	F7
Current owner	Louisiana & Delta 1504
Previous owners	Cadillac & Lake City 48; Railroad Inc.
Notes	Named "Patoutville"; has Operation Lifesaver markings

2488

Rebuild Date	12/74
F-unit no.	337L
F-unit type	F7
Current owner	Keokuk Junction 488
Previous owners	NRE

2487

Rebuild Date	12/74
F-unit no.	342L
F-unit type	F7
Current owner	Gloster Southern 1501
Previous owners	
Notes	Rebuilt by AD&N 6/86

2486

Rebuild Date	1/75
F-unit no.	259C
F-unit type	F7
Current owner	Pee Dee River 2486
Previous owners	Aberdeen & Rockfish 2486; Blue Mountain & Reading

2485

Rebuild Date	1/75
F-unit no.	289C
F-unit type	F9
Current owner	Indiana Rail Road 2485
Previous owners	
Notes	Wrecked, used for parts

2484

Rebuild Date	1/75
F-unit no.	241L
F-unit type	F7
Current owner	Minnesota Commercial 484
Previous owners	NRE
Notes	Named "City of Bayport"

2483

Rebuild Date	1/75
F-unit no.	224C
F-unit type	F7
Current owner	Columbus & Greenville 808
Previous owners	National Railway Equipment

2482

Rebuild Date	1/75
F-unit no.	284L
F-unit type	F9
Current owner	Chattooga & Chickamauga 103
Previous owners	Columbus & Greenville 810; National Railway Equipment

2481

Rebuild Date	1/76
F-unit no.	250L
F-unit type	F7
Current owner	Red River Valley & Western 302
Previous owners	National Railway Equipment; trade-in to GE

2480

Rebuild Date	2/76
F-unit no.	286L
F-unit type	F9
Current owner	Clinton Terminal 2480
Previous owners	Waccamaw Coast Line 2480; Blue Mountain & Reading

2479

Rebuild Date	3/76
F-unit no.	286C
F-unit type	F9
Current owner	Thomas Steel Corp. 2479
Previous owners	

2478

Rebuild Date	6/76
F-unit no.	226C
F-unit type	F7
Current owner	Econo-Rail 2478
Previous owners	

2477

Rebuild Date	8/76
F-unit no.	225C
F-unit type	F7
Current owner	Rail Link 477
Previous owners	Carolina & Northwestern 477; Nashville & Eastern 2477; Tennken

2476

Rebuild Date	9/76
F-unit no.	207C
F-unit type	F7
Current owner	Delta Southern 103
Previous owners	NRE

2475

Rebuild Date	10/76
F-unit no.	263L
F-unit type	F7
Current owner	Rail Link 475
Previous owners	Nashville & Eastern 2475; Tennken

2474

Rebuild Date	11/76
F-unit no.	281C
F-unit type	F9
Current owner	Florida Central 47
Previous owners	Florida Central 2474

2473

Rebuild Date	12/76
F-unit no.	345C (301C)
F-unit type	F7
Current owner	Econo-Rail 2473
Previous owners	
Notes	Was leased to Fort Worth & Western 2473

2472

Rebuild Date	12/76
F-unit no.	238L
F-unit type	F7
Current owner	IMC Fertilizer 204
Previous owners	NRE; Blue Mountain & Reading; trade-in to GE

2471

Rebuild Date	2/77
F-unit no.	281L
F-unit type	F9
Current owner	Louisiana & Delta 1503
Previous owners	Falls Creek 2471; Blue Mountain & Reading; trade-in to GE

2470

Rebuild Date	2/77
F-unit no.	339L
F-unit type	F7
Current owner	Louisiana & Delta 1502
Previous owners	Buffalo & Pittsburgh 2470; Falls Creek 2470; Blue Mountain & Reading; trade-in to GE

2469

Rebuild Date	2/77
F-unit no.	265C
F-unit type	F7
Current owner	IMC 215
Previous owners	Silcott; DuPont 2469; Blue Mountain & Reading; trade-in to GE

2468

Rebuild Date	3/77
F-unit no.	341L
F-unit type	F7
Current owner	Red River Valley & Western 308
Previous owners	NRE; trade-in to GE

2467

Rebuild Date	3/77
F-unit no.	247L
F-unit type	F7
Current owner	Red River Valley & Western 307
Previous owners	National Railway Equipment; trade-in to GE

2466

Rebuild Date	3/77
F-unit no.	346L(305L)
F-unit type	F7
Current owner	South Dakota Wheat Growers Association 306
Previous owners	Independent Locomotive Services; Red River Valley & Western 306; National Railway Equipment; trade-in to GE

2465

Rebuild Date	3/77
F-unit no.	273L
F-unit type	F7
Current owner	Columbus & Greenville 803
Previous owners	National Railway Equipment; trade-in to GE

2464

Rebuild Date	3/77
F-unit no.	345L (308L)
F-unit type	F7
Current owner	Columbus & Greenville 804
Previous owners	Chattooga & Chickamauga 102; Columbus & Greenville 804; NRE; trade-in to GE

2463

Rebuild Date	4/77
F-unit no.	338L
F-unit type	F7
Current owner	Amtrak 591
Previous owners	

2462

Rebuild Date	4/77
F-unit no.	340L
F-unit type	F7
Current owner	
Previous owners	Amtrak 590

2461

Rebuild Date	5/77
F-unit no.	232C
F-unit type	F7
Current owner	
Previous owners	Amtrak 589
Notes	Retired & sold

2460

Rebuild Date	5/77
F-unit no.	283C
F-unit type	F9
Current owner	Naporano Iron & Metal
Previous owners	Amtrak 588

2459

Rebuild Date	5/77
F-unit no.	288C
F-unit type	F9
Current owner	Amtrak 587
Previous owners	

LEFT: Formerly Nashville & Eastern 2477 (originally Santa Fe 2477), the Carolina & Northwestern 477 is now painted in the Rail Link corporate scheme. Rail Link is now owned by Genesee & Wyoming, who possesses a substantial fleet of CF7's. The logo on the back of the engine says, "Stay on track. Don't get Railroaded into Drugs." This slogan can be found on other Rail Link locomotives as well. Photo by Cary F. Poole.

RIGHT: Mass Central 2443 exemplifies what a good coat of paint can do for a locomotive! The 2443 exhibits the extra side cab window and the smaller extra front window to give the engineer better visibility. Early in 1993, the locomotive left to work on the nearby Bay Colony Railroad on a lease/buy option. The Bay Colony has since purchased the unit. Photo taken at Palmer, Massachusetts, in January 1991, by Robert A. LaMay.

BELOW: In February 1993, Mass Central 2443 shows off her beautiful colors at Palmer, Massachusetts. Note the "blatt" horn, the firecracker antenna and the extra cab window on the side. Photo by Robert A. LaMay.

ABOVE: Mexicana De Cobre 2431 poses for the camera on January 18, 1989. Notice how similar it is to Nittany & Bald Eagle 2429 -- each locomotive has the extra cab windows on the side and front, the "blatt" horns, a/c and ground plates are all situated the same and both have four stacks. Look at the number boards on the Mexican unit -- the background color matches the color of the lettering and striping. This unit, along with 2423 were painted for Mexicana De Cobre at Cleburne. The shop personnel remember the units leaving looking like this and heading straight for Laredo. Photograph by Dick Campbell.

BELOW: The Nittany & Bald Eagle painted one of their CF7's in this striking scheme of Midnight blue with white script lettering and trim and the silver trucks are very striking, as well. This unit eventually was traded, along with the 2444, to Conrail, who actually owned these two CF7's before dealing them to the Reading & Northern as their 1503 and 1504. Photographed May 16, 1988, at Bellefonte, Pennsylvania, by Michael Herman, collection of H.E. Brouse.

2458

Rebuild Date	5/77
F unit no.	332L (313L)
F-unit type	F7
Current owner	Scrapped
Previous owners	
Notes	Damaged by fire and scrapped at Cleburne Shops

2457

Rebuild Date	5/77
F-unit no.	246L
F-unit type	F7
Current owner	Amtrak 586
Previous owners	

2456

Rebuild Date	5/77
F-unit no.	215C
F-unit type	F7
Current owner	Amtrak 585
Previous owners	
Notes	Air tanks moved to roof to make room for HEP; HEP never installed

2455

Rebuild Date	6/77
F-unit no.	252L
F-unit type	F7
Current owner	Scrapped
Previous owners	
Notes	Southwest Railway Car Parts

2454

Rebuild Date	6/77
F-unit no.	210C
F-unit type	F7
Current owner	
Previous owners	Amtrak 584
Notes	Retired & sold

2453

Rebuild Date	6/77
F-unit no.	237C
F-unit type	F7
Current owner	Amtrak 583
Previous owners	

2452

Rebuild Date	6/77
F-unit no.	258C
F-unit type	F7
Current owner	Econo-Rail 2452
Previous owners	

2451

Rebuild Date	7/77
F-unit no.	234L
F-unit type	F7
Current owner	Columbus & Greenville 802
Previous owners	NRE; trade-in to GE

2450

Rebuild Date	7/77
F-unit no.	254C
F-unit type	F7
Current owner	Columbus & Greenville 801
Previous owners	National Railway Equipment; trade-in to GE

2449

Rebuild Date	7/77
F-unit no.	259L
F-unit type	F7
Current owner	Nashville & Eastern 2449
Previous owners	Tennken

2448

Rebuild Date	7/77
F-unit no.	334L (315L)
F-unit type	F7
Current owner	Red River Valley & Western 301
Previous owners	NRE

2447

Rebuild Date	8/77
F-unit no.	212L
F-unit type	F7
Current owner	Texas Industries Cement Inc.
Previous owners	

2446

Rebuild Date	8/77
F-unit no.	261C
F-unit type	F7
Current owner	Reading & Northern 1502
Previous owners	Blue Mountain Reading & Northern 601; trade-in to GE
Notes	Retired

2445

Rebuild Date	8/77
F-unit no.	208L
F-unit type	F7
Current owner	Amtrak 582
Previous owners	

2444

Rebuild Date	8/77
F-unit no.	331L (307C) (43C)
F-unit type	F7
Current owner	Reading & Northern 1504
Previous owners	Conrail 44; North Shore/ Stourbridge/ Nittany & Bald Eagle 44; Blue Mountain & Reading

2443

Rebuild Date	8/77
F-unit no.	333L (306L)
F-unit type	F7
Current owner	Bay Colony 2443
Previous owners	Massachusetts Central; Blue Mountain & Reading
Notes	BCLR leased from MCER on a lease/buy option, now owns

2442

Rebuild Date	8/77
F-unit no.	325L (306L:1)
F-unit type	F7
Current owner	South Kansas & Oklahoma 106
Previous owners	Meridian & Bigbee 106; NRE; trade-in to GE

2441

Rebuild Date	9/77
F-unit no.	287C
F-unit type	F9
Current owner	Chevron
Previous owners	WATCO 4
Notes	Previously leased to ASARCO

2440

Rebuild Date	9/77
F-unit no.	269C
F-unit type	F7
Current owner	
Previous owners	Amtrak 581
Notes	Retired & sold

2439

Rebuild Date	9/77
F-unit no.	258L
F-unit type	F7
Current owner	
Previous owners	Amtrak 580
Notes	Retired & sold

2438

Rebuild Date	9/77
F-unit no.	237L
F-unit type	F7
Current owner	Naporano Iron & Metal
Previous owners	Amtrak 579

2437

Rebuild Date	10/77
F-unit no.	275C
F-unit type	F7
Current owner	Independent Locomotive Svcs.
Previous owners	Amtrak 578
Notes	Scrapped, prime mover was removed and placed in RETX 302, a GP9

2436

Rebuild Date	10/77
F-unit no.	285C
F-unit type	F9
Current owner	Scrapped
Previous owners	
Notes	Southwest Railway Car Parts

2435

Rebuild Date	10/77
F-unit no.	329L (310L)
F-unit type	F7
Current owner	Scrapped
Previous owners	
Notes	Metal Processing Industries

2434

Rebuild Date	10/77
F-unit no.	285L
F-unit type	F9
Current owner	Columbus & Greenville 805
Previous owners	National Railway Equipment; trade-in to GE

2433

Rebuild Date	11/77
F-unit no.	263C
F-unit type	F7
Current owner	
Previous owners	Amtrak 577
Notes	Retired & sold

2432

Rebuild Date	11/77
F-unit no.	288L
F-unit type	F9
Current owner	Newton Asphalt
Previous owners	Blue Mountain & Reading

LEFT: Columbus & Greenville #802 has a restenciled Santa Fe Warbonnet scheme in this view taken at Leeland, Mississippi, in Fall of 1990. Note that the extra engineer's extra front window has been plated over. Photograph by Tom Sink.

2431
Rebuild Date	12/77
F-unit no.	235C
F-unit type	F7
Current owner	Mexicana De Cobre 2431
Previous owners	

2430
Rebuild Date	12/77
F-unit no.	227C
F-unit type	F7
Current owner	Naporano Iron & Metal
Previous owners	Amtrak 576

2429
Rebuild Date	12/77
F-unit no.	236C
F-unit type	F7
Current owner	Reading & Northern 1503
Previous owners	Conrail 2429; Nittany & Bald Eagle 2429; Blue Mountain & Reading 2429

2428
Rebuild Date	12/77
F-unit no.	274C
F-unit type	F7
Current owner	Texas Industries Cement 2428
Previous owners	

2427
Rebuild Date	12/77
F-unit no.	268L
F-unit type	F7
Current owner	Nittany & Bald Eagle 2427
Previous owners	Blue Mountain & Reading

2426
Rebuild Date	1/78
F-unit no.	330L
F-unit type	F7
Current owner	Maryland & Pennsylvania 1502
Previous owners	Rail System Inc.
Notes	Used by NYS&W prior to sale to MPA

2425
Rebuild Date	1/78
F-unit no.	261L
F-unit type	F7
Current owner	Maryland & Pennsylvania 1504
Previous owners	Rail System Inc.
Notes	Used by NYS&W prior to sale to MPA

2424
Rebuild Date	1/78
F-unit no.	335L
F-unit type	F7
Current owner	Reading & Northern 1501
Previous owners	Blue Mountain & Reading 600; Blue Mountain & Reading 424; trade-in to GE
Notes	Retired

2423
Rebuild Date	1/78
F-unit no.	215L
F-unit type	F7
Current owner	Mexicana De Cobre 2423
Previous owners	

2422
Rebuild Date	1/78
F-unit no.	245L
F-unit type	F7
Current owner	South Dakota Wheat Growers Association 300
Previous owners	Red River Valley & Western 300; NRE; trade-in to GE

2421
Rebuild Date	2/78
F-unit no.	252C
F-unit type	F7
Current owner	Black River & Western 42
Previous owners	NRE; trade-in to GE

2420
Rebuild Date	2/78
F-unit no.	238L (309L
F-unit type	F7
Current owner	Allegheny 112
Previous owners	Blue Mountain & Reading; trade-in to GE
Notes	For parts

2419
Rebuild Date	3/78
F-unit no.	326L (307L)
F-unit type	F7
Current owner	Black River & Western 41
Previous owners	Blue Mountain & Reading; trade-in to GE
Notes	Scrapped

2418
Rebuild Date	3/78
F-unit no.	260C
F-unit type	F7
Current owner	
Previous owners	Amtrak 575
Notes	Retired & sold

2417
Rebuild Date	3/78
F-unit no.	275L
F-unit type	F7
Current owner	Yorkrail 1500
Previous owners	Maryland & Pennsylvania 1500 / Emons Transportation 1500; Rail System Inc.
Notes	Used by NYS&W prior to sale to Emons

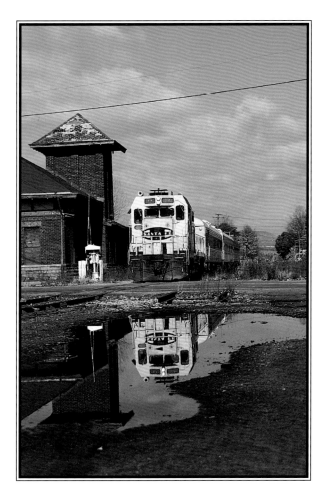

LEFT: The New York, Susquehanna & Western leased three CF7's from Rail System, Inc., but did not touch them with paint; they ran in full ATSF dress their entire time on the NYS&W, before being sold to Emons Transportation. Here, the 2425 is hauling a charter passenger train southbound from Jamesville, New York, in late 1986. The unit would eventually become MPA 1504. Photo by Jaime F.M. Serensits.

BELOW: The Black River & Western 42 was originally the ATSF 2421, and was painted into this attractive scheme and modified in 1995. Modifications included the placement of the horns on a bracket on the upper part of the long hood on the fireman's side. Unit is shown switching the Union Carbide plant at Bound Brook, New Jersey, an assignment that it no longer holds. Photograph taken Spring 1996 by Gary Kazin.

BOTTOM: BR&W's 41 received an early repaint into green and yellow, and ran for several years before being cannibalized for parts. It was scrapped in 1995. On November 4, 1984, however, the 41 was in charge of a passenger run photographed by Thomas Horvath.

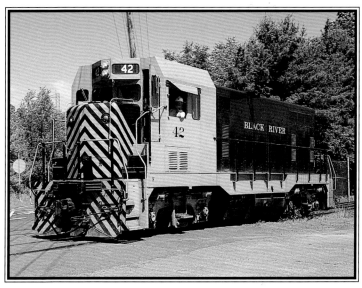

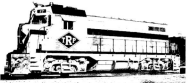

WARBONNETS

ABOVE: Four Midwest Coal Handlers CF7's roll a loaded coal train past the enormous cooling towers of the U.S. Tennessee Valley Authority Paradise Steam Plant in Drakesboro, Kentucky, on November 22, 1992. Included in this consist are 2627 (the only two-stacker in the bunch), 2508 (with remote control lights), 2511 (our former movie star, now scrapped) and 2495. They all carry a unique version of the warbonnet, not likely to be confused with any other railroad. Photo by Kel Aiken.

ABOVE: The Los Angeles Junction has always been a wholly-owned subsidiary of the Santa Fe. Long after ATSF unloaded their last CF7, the LAJ soldiers on with an armada of CF7's looking very much like the diesels of their parent company. The Scotchlite outlining the initials on the long hood is a nice touch. Unit retains its original two-stack configuration. Photo by Kel Aiken at Los Angeles Junction, California, on October 28, 1993.

LEFT: Wearing a thin disguise, it is not difficult to tell that North Shore 44 formerly belonged to the Santa Fe. This former-ATSF CF7 #2444 is now operated by the Reading & Northern in the same paint, but wearing the road number 1504. Photographed at Northumberland, Pennsylvania, on November 17, 1985, by H.E. Brouse.

A New Beginning

It is with dedication to their craft from the men and women of the Cleburne Shop, that so many CF7's are still operating on a daily basis 20-25 years after their rebuild took place. The CF7 is arguably the short-line locomotive of the 1990's.

The CF7 locomotive served the Santa Fe for 17 years as both a road unit and a switcher. The #2649 served fourteen years before it left the roster and the newest unit, the #2417 served six years before being sold off.

The CF7's found themselves in the same position as had the F7. More modern, powerful locomotives were needed and the decision was made to phase the units from the rosters. Units with only 1500 horsepower were no longer needed by the railroad. It was simply a matter of the Santa Fe needing higher horsepower units.

The Santa Fe may have received a harbinger of things to come with shortlines when a Mexican copper mining company approached them with an offer to buy two units. With the company willing to pay cash, the two units left Cleburne numbered 2431 and 2423, lettered for Mexicana de Cobre, and painted in a gray with black trim paint scheme. The units entered Mexico by traveling over the International Bridge at Laredo, Texas.

With the explosion of shortlines in the early 1980's, Santa Fe found eager takers. The sell-off began in 1984, and by 1987, most were off the property and in the hands of shortlines. Cleburne found itself with a long line of CF7's in 1986, all being offered for sale to whomever would take them. Most of the CF7's have now had several owners, and even as such, more often than not, you will find one of these units hard at work in an industrial setting. As mentioned in the Introduction, Mr. Russell Tedder of the Ashley, Drew & Northern Railroad visited the Cleburne Shops in 1986 and found a long line of CF7 locomotives for sale. Tedder had brought along his Chief Mechanical Officer, and the two men carefully inspect-ed the units and picked out four locomotives, two for the Gloster & Southern and two for the Ashley, Drew & Northern. The Santa Fe was eager to deal; the sale included a new paint job for the locomotives at a bargain price. The units were painted in the classic green and white paint scheme for which the AD&N is known, but the units arrived in Arkansas unlettered because the Santa Fe did not have stencils to do the lettering.

In October 1988, CF7 #50 of the Cadillac & Lake City Railroad was featured in a television cigarette commercial which was produced for Mexican markets. The commercial featured a young lady in a white Cadillac and a guy on a Harley-Davidson with a freight train coming between the two as they sat on opposite sides of the track. Open box-cars allowed the two to see each other and after the train passes, the man hands the woman a Lucky Strike cigarette. After a quick paint job of bright red on the cab and blue on the long hood, the commercial was com-

BELOW: A former Santa Fe 2476 and another CF7 at Cleburne shops. Santa Fe name on nose and long hood are white-lined, as are the numbers on the cab & in the number boards. A small "NREC" is stenciled on cab. The 2476 will eventually become Delta Southern 103. Photo by Bob Leverknight.

Laid-up Good Order "L.U.G.O." list given to prospective customers visiting Cleburne... a "locomotive shopping list", if you will. L.U.G.O is a report generated by the Santa Fe to help clients select the CF7 that's just right for them.

CF7 LOCOMOTIVES IN L.U.G.O. STATUS BY CLASS III MILEAGE ORDER 1

13:57 THURSDAY, MARCH 22, 1984

OBS	ck 1 Orig New	UNITNO	CLASS	ck 2 Remfg	TRAINSYM	CLS3MILE	CLS3DATE	LUGDATE
1	8-51	2649	2417	2-70	ONHANDLUGO	137844	7810	811118
2	12-49	2645	2417	10-70	ONHANDLUGO	153044	7809	811119
3	12-53	2562	2417	7-73	ONHANDLUGO	157127	7811	811114
4	9-49	2595	2417	11-72	ONHANDLUGO	166507	7807	811114
5	12-53	2584	2417	1-73	ONHANDLUGO	170753	7808	811218
6	10-52	2531	2417	3-74	ONHANDLUGO	180537	8403	811114
7	7-49	2587	2417	1-73	ONHANDLUGO	180948	7809	820723
8	12-49	2513	2417	7-74	ONHANDLUGO	191253	8407	820421
9	9-49	2594	2417	11-72	ONHANDLUGO	191547	7802	811114
10	11-53	2428	2417	12-77	ONHANDLUGO	197571	7712	811227
11	3-50	2592	2417	11-72	ONHANDLUGO	197650	7802	811114
12	10-52	2632	2417	12-71	ONHANDLUGO	198517	7711	811114
13	4-50	2432	2417	12-77	ONHANDLUGO	200365	7711	821124
14	12-53	2514	2417	12-77	ONHANDLUGO	207757	8407	820725
15	11-49	2447	2417	8-77	ONHANDLUGO	210747	7708	820106
16	8-49	2445	2417	8-77	ONHANDLUGO	213424	7708	820723
17	3-50	2430	2417	12-77	ONHANDLUGO	215228	7712	821121
18	8-51	2418	2417	3-78	ONHANDLUGO	217018	7803	821117
19	5-51	2421	2417	2-78	ONHANDLUGO	218877	7802	821121
20	11-53	2463	2417	1-71	ONHANDLUGO	221068	7704	820728
21	2-51	2457	2417	5-77	ONHANDLUGO	221278	7705	811218
22	5-51	2521	2417	5-74	ONHANDLUGO	224215	8404	820729
23	11-49	2423	2417	1-78	ONHANDLUGO	224508	7801	821123
24	4-50	2451	2417	11-77	ONHANDLUGO	224954	7707	820922
25	2-51	2422	2417	1-78	ONHANDLUGO	227830	7801	821121
26	4-50	2453	2417	6-77	ONHANDLUGO	229857	7706	820724
27	11-53	2417	2417	3-78	ONHANDLUGO	230105	7803	821121
28	5-50	2426	2417	1-78	ONHANDLUGO	231144	7801	821124
29	9-51	2427	2417	12-77	ONHANDLUGO	233862	7712	821121
30	5-50	2419	2417	3-78	ONHANDLUGO	234431	7803	821121
31	4-50	2438	2417	9-77	ONHANDLUGO	237094	7709	821121
32	6-51	2424	2417	1-78	ONHANDLUGO	238969	7801	821121
33	5-50	2420	2417	2-78	ONHANDLUGO	239480	7802	821117
34	4-50	2574	2417	4-78	ONHANDLUGO	240879	7709	820723
35	11-49	2456	2417	5-77	ONHANDLUGO	240979	7706	820722
36	7-49	2454	2417	6-77	ONHANDLUGO	240987	7706	820726
37	8-51	2425	2417	8-78	ONHANDLUGO	241250	7801	821125
38	6-56	2434	2417	10-77	ONHANDLUGO	241601	7710	821122
39	3-50	2461	2417	4-77	ONHANDLUGO	243230	7704	820722
40	11-53	2440	2417	9-77	ONHANDLUGO	244028	7709	821119
41	10-52	2444	2417	8-77	ONHANDLUGO	244371	7708	820722
42	5-51	2439	2417	9-77	ONHANDLUGO	244468	7709	821121
43	5-51	2450	2417	7-77	ONHANDLUGO	244904	7707	820722
44	2-51	2468	2417	3-77	ONHANDLUGO	245367	7703	820721
45	5-53	2462	2417	4-77	ONHANDLUGO	246288	7704	820724
46	11-53	2437	2417	10-77	ONHANDLUGO	246676	7710	821121
47	5-50	2442	2417	8-77	ONHANDLUGO	247403	7708	821121
48	8-51	2446	2417	8-77	ONHANDLUGO	248467	7708	820721
49	8-51	2433	2417	11-77	ONHANDLUGO	251111	7711	821122
50	11-53	2588	2417	1-73	ONHANDLUGO	251469	7702	811218
51	10-49	2466	2417	3-77	ONHANDLUGO	252284	7703	820722
52	6-51	2448	2417	7-77	ONHANDLUGO	252575	7707	820724
53	12-52	2464	2417	3-77	ONHANDLUGO	255073	7703	820725
54	11-53	2465	2417	3-77	ONHANDLUGO	257844	7703	820722
55	5-53	2470	2417	2-77	ONHANDLUGO	258798	7702	820728
56	9-51	2469	2417	2-77	ONHANDLUGO	260186	7702	820727
57	4-50	2431	2417	12-78	ONHANDLUGO	260411	7712	821124
58	4-50	2429	2417	12-77	ONHANDLUGO	260900	7712	821124
59	12-52	2443	2417	8-77	ONHANDLUGO	263983	7708	821121
60	5-56	2460	2417	5-77	ONHANDLUGO	264831	7705	820729
61	7-56	2459	2417	5-77	ONHANDLUGO	266188	7705	820724
62	6-56	2471	2417	2-77	ONHANDLUGO	266603	7702	820729
63	4-50	2472	2417	12-76	ONHANDLUGO	270622	7612	820724
64	4-53	2500	2417	9-74	ONHANDLUGO	275813	8409	820721
65	2-51	2467	2417	3-77	ONHANDLUGO	277721	7703	820721

after 12-1-78 ~~beginning~~
26-L was applied

CF7 FLEETS

ABOVE: In new platinum mist paint, an Amtrak CF7 awaits a call to duty at Amtrak's Chicago diesel shop. Amtrak's 585 has been heavily modified for use in the Windy City. The engineer's side has an all-weather window installed, a red beacon was placed above the headlights, strobes were added to the roof of the cab and air tanks relocated to the top of the long hood. The tanks were moved in order to make room for a Head End Power generator, but it was never installed. The HEP was to be placed there in case the 585 was ever called to go out and rescue a stranded train. It was formerly Santa Fe 2456. There are rumored connections between the box leaning against the engineer's window, the food on the ground and the pigeon. Photographed by Steve Smedley on April 1, 1985.

ABOVE: Amtrak 577 leads a pumpkin and two ballast cars at the old New Haven Railroad coaling tower in the Cedar Hill Yard at New Haven, Connecticut, in July, 1985. Notice that the cab roof has been entirely cleared -- horn relocated to front of cab, air conditioner and ground plane removed. This was due to clearance concerns on the North East Corridor where these units operated. Photos above and left by Robert A. LaMay.

LEFT: Amtrak 576 (former ATSF 2430) and another CF7 are in charge of a ballast train at Old Saybrook, Connecticut, in October 1990. The 576 sports a decal honoring Amtrak's Boston Division Mechanical Department. Also take note of shamrock painted on the buffer plate and that the small extra window for the engineer has been plated over. A closer inspection reveals that the engineer's rear view mirror is missing.

ABOVE: Trying hard to match the colors of Reading & Northern's CF7 #1502, the sky above Reading, Pennsylvania, is putting on quite a show. The 1502 was formerly Blue Mountain & Reading #601, which was originally ATSF #2446. Notice that the 1502 still retains its "blatt" horn on the fireman's side. The 1502 and 1501 were involved in a wreck in 1996, in which both received severe-enough damage to be retired. Photo by Jaime F.M. Serensits.

ABOVE: Blue Mountain & Reading 601 shows off its beautiful purple paint. It is one of the few CF7's that displayed its model designation under the road number below the cab window. The ground plane is very prominent from this angle. Photographed on April 26, 1986, at Hamburg, Pennsylvania, by H. E. Brouse.

RIGHT: Blue Mountain & Reading 600 wears a banner and flags celebrating the inauguration of scheduled passenger excursion service during the summer of 1985. The 600 and 601 handled the southbound train out of South Hamburg, and met the northbound train from Temple at Leesport. The northbound train was pulled by Canadian Pacific Hudson 4-6-4 number 2839. At Leesport a golden spike ceremony was held. The 600 had been renumbered from BM&R 424, which was originally Santa Fe 2424. It later became R&N 1501. Photo by Allen Keller.

pleted and the #50 was returned to its owners. Today, this locomotive works as the #50 on the Florida Northern Railroad.

CF7 #2511 was painted for a fictitious railroad in 1977 to star in a made-for-television movie. The make-believe railroad, the "Milwaukee & Northern," was featured in the movie, "Man With The Power." The Santa Fe oval sported the name "Milwaukee & Northern", which was also applied down the long hood.

With several years having passed from the rebuild program, one particular problem does exist with the CF7. As many would suspect, the problem has to do with the sagging of the frame. Mr. Eldon Whitworth noted early in the program that the change over from Tri-10 steel to a milder form of steel causes the noses to drop on some units. It maybe the changeover is the fault of the frame sag as well. The Tri-10 steel was substituted with 10-40 steel because the Topeka Shops could get it cheaper. The substitution was not communicated to Cleburne and not known until some collisions occurred and the nose or rear on a CF7 would drop. Only after investigating these incidents did Cleburne learn of the substitution.

As the Santa Fe began to sell off the CF7's, it found a ready market in the form of shortlines. The CF7 represented the first Class I rebuild locomotive to make it to the used locomotive market. The Illinois Central cashed in later with its GP8 and GP10 units and CSX has sold many of its GP16's to an eager shortline market. When the Santa Fe began to unload the units, it was reported they could be had as little as $20,000 per unit if purchased through Santa Fe, fully serviced and ready to roll. If purchased through a broker, the cost was upwards of $50,000; however, the condition of the locomotive and market situations could influence the price. Some railroads such as the Indiana Rail Road started service in 1986 with an all-CF7 roster. Incidentally, the Indiana Rail Road has been purchased by CSX, illustrating the CF7's connection with Class I railroads today. Other railroads such as the Delta Southern and GWI currently operate all-CF7 rosters. Other railroads such as the Louisiana & Delta mix mostly CF7's with an occasional Geep.

Amtrak found itself with 25 units numbered 575-599 after a trade with the Santa Fe. Of the 25 units Amtrak received, it was reported that eight of the units were received in their original round roof cabs. In the trade, Santa Fe gave Amtrak 25 CF7's and 18 SSB1200's for a total of 43 locomotives.

The SSB1200's represented another Santa Fe rebuild program which was conducted in San Bernardino, California, which focused on end-cab switchers. The SSB1200 were rated at 1200 horsepower and stood for Switcher-San Bernardino and represented three NW2's, twenty-three SW9's, and 3 SW1200's for a total of 29 units rebuilt. This particular Santa Fe rebuild program lasted from 1973 until 1979, but by the early 1980's, Santa Fe had made a corporate decision to phase out "pure" switchers and go with multiple-use road-switchers.

By the mid-1980's Santa Fe had progressed to a point where it wanted to shed itself of low-horsepower road switchers such as the CF7 as well. What the Santa Fe received in return for the trade to Amtrak were 18 six-axle SDP40F's which were numbered 5250-5267. These units were

ABOVE: Yorkrail 1500, ex-2417, was the last CF7 to roll out of Santa Fe's Cleburne Shops. The unit was previously lettered for parent company, Emons Transportation. In 1996, the unit was repainted into Yorkrail's Operation Lifesaver scheme. For a short time in the interim, it was pressed into service unlettered (see photo on page 101). Later that year, the nose emblem was added to commemorate Emons' 25th anniversary in 1997. Photo taken at Medusa Minerals facility at Thomasville, Pennsylvania, on October 15, 1996, by Jaime F.M. Serensits.

MODIFICATIONS

ABOVE: Black River & Western #42 works at the Union Carbide plant in Bound Brook, New Jersey. BRW has modified their CF7, including putting number boards and classification lights on the rear of the unit (to match their GP9 and GP7's), and changing the bell placement to the brakeman's side of the long hood. They also added a plug-in cord which charges the batteries and keeps the engine warm. Photographed early Summer 1996 by Gary Kazin.

BELOW: Another CF7 that has been modified is the IMC 215, ex-Dupont 2469, photographed at the facility in Noralyn, Florida, on February 25, 1996. The shields are to protect the fans from falling rocks. Photo by James F. Reed.

WINDOWS

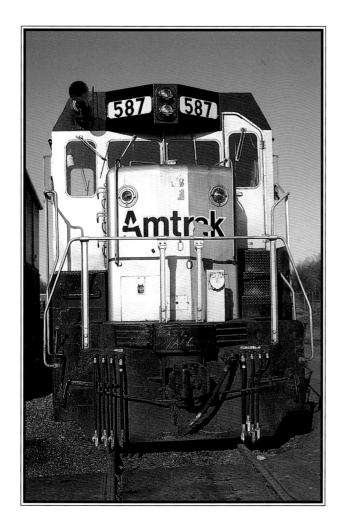

LEFT: Amtrak 587, formerly Santa Fe 2459, shows off the original engineer's window size and placement. Also notice unique placement of horn "sticking out of the engineer's head." Some wag apparently dubbed the 587 the "Fast Mail", according to the moniker scribed on the buffer plate. Photo taken at Rensselear, New York, in January 1993, by Robert A. LaMay.

BELOW LEFT: Blue Mountain & Reading 424 shows the second variation of the engineer's front window arrangement. At the request of crews, this second window was added at knee level to enhance the engineer's view of a crew member working on the ground. Some railroads later plated these windows over (see AMTK 576 on page 76). Photo taken by Jay Leinbach at South Hamburg, Pennsylvania, in Spring 1985.

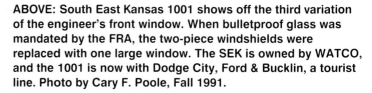

ABOVE: South East Kansas 1001 shows off the third variation of the engineer's front window. When bulletproof glass was mandated by the FRA, the two-piece windshields were replaced with one large window. The SEK is owned by WATCO, and the 1001 is now with Dodge City, Ford & Bucklin, a tourist line. Photo by Cary F. Poole, Fall 1991.

Two views of Red River Valley & Western CF7's at Breckenridge, Minnesota. At one time, the RRV&W had a fleet of 10 CF7's; the #300 and #306 are now owned by South Dakota Wheat Growers Association. RRV&W #309 is currently getting "slugged" at RRV&W's sister company, Twin Cities & Western, which may use the unit. These views give you a chance to compare two different side cab window and exhaust stack arrangements. The top photo illustrates the forward-sitting window, with the extra window (which is plated-over). The 309 exhibits the centered window arrangement. Note the all-weather windows on each unit. Both photos by Tom Sink.

ABOVE: Inman Locomotive's ISCX 111 in a beautiful Inman scheme, lettered for Seapac, is shown at Inman's Baytown, Texas, facility, where WATCO refurbishes its diesel fleet. Inman is owned by WATCO, who performs contract switching services. The 111 subsequently displayed the word "SEAPAC" spelled-out vertically on the nose. The unit was formerly WATCO 11, ex-2648; note the two stacks. All three of the photos on this page illustrate the punishment that contract locomotives receive; these units leave the Inman facility as practically new locomotives. See photos of WATX 6, 11 and SEK 1001 for examples of standard WATCO power. Photo taken May 5, 1996.

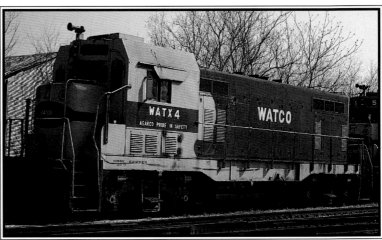

ABOVE: WATX #4 had previously served the Asarco facility at El Paso, Texas. Unit shows signs of heavy use in an industrial setting. Photographed at WATCO's Inman Locomotive facility in Baytown, Texas, on March 17, 1996. Unit has since been sold to Chevron.

LEFT: WATX 55 (formerly WATX 5) had also been assigned to the Asarco plant at El Paso with #4. As recently as March 1996, unit was WATX 5. Note missing pilot, masking tape on window, shop truck up front and primer on engineer's side of front of unit... locomotive will get overhauled and painted before reassignment. It has been outshopped as ISCX 5, but will eventually be repainted for WATCO. Photographed at Baytown, Texas, May 5, 1996. All photos this page by Ted Ferkenhoff.

ABOVE: Econo-Rail 2608 is doing what Econo-Rail does best -- performing contract switching services for large industrial complexes, like this Kraft plant at Sherman, Texas. The 2608 had apparently revisited the Cleburne shops to have its round cab replaced. Even the number boards show a later style of Santa Fe numbers. Photograph taken in late Summer 1993, by Cary F. Poole.

BELOW: Econo-Rail 2452 shows some wear after spending time at North Star Steel at Beaumont, Texas, performing contract switching for Econo-Rail. Notice the "new" section bolted to the pilot of 2452. The "yellow dip" scheme replaces their old blue. The 2452 is an exception; most of Econo-Rail's equipment looks very clean and bright in this new yellow scheme. Photo taken April 9, 1996, by Ted Ferkenhoff.

BELOW: CF7 2511 has been "painted" and properly "weathered" by movie personnel for her starring role in the made-for-television movie, "Man With The Power." This "Milwaukee & Northern" CF7 is seen at San Bernardino, California, on February 22, 1977. Photo by Steve Patterson.

later rebuilt in 1985 at which time front hand rails were added and they were re-geared for freight service. While the number of locomotives seemed slanted to Amtrak's favor, horsepower rating for the traded totaled 59,100 horsepower going to Amtrak and 54,000 going to the Santa Fe. Each railroad got what it needed; Amtrak needed switchers and short-haul units and Santa Fe needed high-horsepower six-axle power. One Amtrak CF7, #585 was even going to be equipped with HEP (head-end power) in order to generate electricity to rescue passenger trains. The air tanks were mounted horizontally on the roof of the long hood and resembled the torpedo racks of early Geeps, but Amtrak later changed its mind and the 585 never received the HEP generator. Of the 25 CF7's received, Amtrak parceled them out to the following locations: 8 to New Haven, Connecticut; 12 to Wilmington, Delaware; 2 to Chicago, Illinois; and 3 to Los Angeles, California. As of February 1,

1997, six units are still on Amtrak's roster and are assigned to the following locations: 2 to Wilmington, Delaware; 2 to Washington, DC; 1 to Sanford, Florida; and 1 to Boston, Massachusetts. The units are used primarily to perform switching duties, pulling work trains and even occasionally serve as a rescue engine for a disabled passenger train.

Railroad equipment groups like National Railway Equipment and Blue Mountain & Reading bought CF7's by the dozen for resale. General Electric even ended up with several units due to trade-ins with Santa Fe and disposed of the units to other railroad equipment companies. A typical method of obtaining a CF7, outside of large companies such as NRE buying them in large numbers, was conducted by the Washington Central Railroad. The Washington Central is a regional railroad formed in 1987 and serves the central portion of Washington. At the suggestion of Red River Valley & Western's president,

Mr. Tom Kotnour, the WCRC's president, Nick Temple, went in search of the units. Mr. Kotnour was a firm believer in the CF7's; he had a fleet of ten on the Red River Valley & Western. With the WCRC fleet of five end-cab switchers and two road switchers being challenged by increased traffic, Mr. Kotnour's recommendation on the units was timely.

Robert Sluys, an electrician for CEECO (Coast Engine & Equipment Company) which maintained WCRC equipment, was dispatched to Barstow, California, to look over ten units which were owned by NRE. What Sluys found were units in varying degrees of service-ability and without any Santa Fe service records to be found. He used his "eyeball judgment" to determine condition on wheels, flanges and so forth. He recommended four units to Nick Temple, who narrowed the choice to two units. The 1987 price tag was $35,000 a unit. The two units later were renumbered #401 (ex-

The CF7 Locomotive

2578) and #402 (ex-2636).

Two companies, Econo-Rail and WATCO bought several units which they either operate themselves in switching service, or lease to customers. Econo-Rail originally purchased 27 CF7's and many still operate in Texas in the Houston and Beaumont areas. Of the 27 owned by Econo-Rail, one was sold to Zacky Farms in California, and seven have been cannibalized to keep the remaining 19 units operating. The 19 CF7's supplement a fleet of 45 locomotives that Econo-Rail uses for contract switching services, locomotive leasing, track construction and repair service.

The Kentucky Railway Museum has the dual distinction of not only being the first historical group to preserve a CF7, #2546, but also their unit still wears a complete Santa Fe paint scheme and has not been renumbered or relettered for any other railroad. The lack of relettering is remarkable for the single fact the unit operated for a period of time on the Indiana Rail Road.

The CF7 on the Kentucky Railway Museum is a favored engine on the line for several reasons. The large cab allows the crew to carry supplies such as chain-saws and other tools for track work. It's large size also permits cab rides for some of the visitors. In training other volunteers for work on the railroad, the unit has very good visibility for the volunteers to learn how to switch and to operate an excursion run. In addition, the unit loads very easily and has good braking capability, qualities much-needed on an excursion railroad. The unit is also noted for its ease of maintenance, on both the prime mover and the generator components, which are easily accessible to the volunteers.

As this book goes to press in early 1997, it is ironic that a handful of CF7's that have ended up on Class I railroads. When the KCS purchased MidSouth in 1994, it found itself with 15 of the units. The KCS prefers units with a 645 versus a 567 prime mover. The KCS also stocks few if any parts for the 567 prime mover employed on the CF7, thus forcing the railroad to sell the units off. This will in turn create another round of acquisitions by shortlines. The GWI Switching Services of Dayton, Texas, recently started service with an all CF7 roster, largely due to purchases from KCS. Combined with the 15 CF7's, the MidSouth ended up with a roster of 83 Paducah-rebuilt GP10's, totaling 98 rebuilt locomotives from a fleet of 107.

Since both CF7's and GP10's from the Paducah rebuild program have hit the used locomotive market, many other shortlines have ended up with both types of units. The Georgia-Pacific Railroads, such as the Ashley, Drew & Northern, Gloster & Southern and Fordyce & Princeton, often run freights with both CF7's and GP10's.

With the buy-back of the Washington Central early in 1997, the BNSF found itself with the two CF7's owned by WCRC. Technically the Santa Fe always retained four CF7's, since it is the sole owner of the Los Angeles Junction Railroad.

As with many locomotive types, the CF7's had several monikers placed on the units. As stated earlier, some railfans referred to the units as simply ugly, but names for the units became even more specific. One person remembered a CF7 being referred to as a "Cleburne bullhead", which was later shortened to "bullhead". This is an apparent reference to the large cab. Other comments centered on being an "ugly duckling" or "cheap geep." However, the Washington Central had probably the most distinctive and accepted (by the locals and men on the railroad) nickname. When referring to the units on this particular railroad, the two units, #401 and #402, were referred to simply as "Hooters". Apparently Bob Sluys had named each of the locomotives used by the Washington Central after a regionally popular music group called "The Hooters". The group got its name from the melodica, a flute-like instrument similar to a recorder which is known in some parts of the country as a hooter. Fred Spurrell, an early researcher on the CF7 program, authored a booklet titled, "From Streamliners, To Bullheads to Hooters," in which details the naming of the units and the loving care given to the railroad's two CF7's. The booklet chronicled the acquisition of two CF7's on the Washington Central Railroad.

ABOVE: The only CF7 to remain in its original Santa Fe paint with no other markings, as well as the only one preserved, is seen here at the Kentucky Railway Museum in New Haven, Kentucky. Unit is used on passenger excursions, and is a favorite of crewmembers there. Photo courtesy of John Campbell of the Kentucky Railway Museum.

ABOVE: Pioneer Valley's Display Train for Railfan Weekend in Westfield, Massachusetts, in July 1989. Note the two different style of number boards, both left over from the Santa Fe. The 2597 displays the older style. Photo by Robert A. LaMay.

LEFT: Florida Northern 50 was originally number 2509 on the Santa Fe, then ran on the Cadillac & Lake City as 2509 and then 50. The silver air conditioner is very apparent in this photo, as well as the set of chimes up front. Less obvious is the set of horns on the rear rooftop, at the back of the long hood. Photograph taken at Ocala, Florida, by Tom Sink.

RIGHT: Looking much like her FNRR sister, Florida Central 49 (former ATSF 2494) sports a slightly different paint scheme, including a different logo placed aside the number, instead of next to the cab window, and the air conditioner is red, while the horns are black. Both units have four stacks and horns on the front and rear. Photo at Wildwood, Florida, on February 20, 1994 by Stanley H. Jackowski, from the collection of Robert A. LaMay.

The CF7 Locomotive

ABOVE: Florida Midland 63 exhibits a variation on the Pinsly family colors at Winter Haven, Florida, on May 22, 1994. This unit's highlights include horns on the front and back, two exhaust stacks and the yellow and red striping around the buffer plate and anti-climber on the pilot. Photo by Stanley H. Jackowski, collection of Robert A. LaMay.

BELOW: Great view shows off Pioneer Valley's 2565 at Westfield, Massachusetts, in December, 1987. Horn placement, air conditioner and ground plane with low-profile antenna are easily located. Also note base for mounting a warning beacon. It looks like that this unit was recently sanded, judging from light-colored material on the nose. Robert A. LaMay photo.

ABOVE: It looks like MidSouth 7001, but it is actually Eastern Illinois Railroad #7001. EIRC never touched the former MidSouth unit with a paint brush the entire time it was on their railroad. The 7001 was later replaced with a couple of Geeps. Photographed at Charleston, Illinois, on May 29, 1993, by Steve Smedley.

OPPOSITE: Florida Central #49 basks in the sunshine at Leesburg, Florida, on February 25, 1996. Note the elongated engineer's front window. Photo by Jay Reed.

RIGHT: Former MidSouth 7003 rests at New Iberia, Louisiana, on December 3, 1995. The MidSouth lettering has been covered, but the old number remains; it currently belongs to the Louisiana & Delta, and will become their 1508. Photo by Bill Lang.

BELOW: The outline of Pike's Peak gives this unit away as having belonged to the Cadillac & Lake City Railroad. It was their number 48. Their other CF7, the 50, went to Florida Northern. The 1504 now wears the Operation Lifesaver emblem for the Louisiana & Delta. Photo taken at Baldwin, Louisiana, on April 29, 1994, by Louis R. Saillard.

BOTTOM: Louisiana & Delta 1501, the "City of New Iberia", appears to be readied in the "launch" position at L&D's shops at New Iberia, Louisiana, on February 16, 1989. A sturdy support of bracing material substitutes for the front truck. Genesee & Wyoming's corporate scheme looks pretty good on the 1501, don't you agree? Photo by Louis R. Saillard.

       The CF7 Locomotive

ABOVE: The 1507, "Breaux Bridge", and former-Allegheny 303 sit nose-to-nose at Schriever, Louisiana, on November 14, 1995. The two ex-Allegheny CF7's, 303 and 304, are still in their blue-with-orange-trim scheme and compliment the bright orange L&D CF7's very well. Notice ditch lights installed on the rear of 1507. Photo by Bill Lang.

BELOW: Round cab pauses next to square cab at Louisiana and Delta's New Iberia facility. Notice that the 304 has the main cab window close to the front edge of the cab and an extra side window, while the 1507 has more of a centered side window without the extra window behind it. Notice also the differences in the louvered panels along the cab. Photo taken New Years Day, 1997, by Mike Zollitsch.

Generally, the CF7 is highly regarded by shortline operators who have placed the locomotive under severe tests. In many instances, the locomotives have performed beyond expectations the Santa Fe would have imposed on it. But when your motive power pool is limited, as on most shortlines, you do what you must do to keep the freight rolling.

One railroad, the Delta Southern which operates from Tallulah, Louisiana, to McGehee, Arkansas, does so with an entire CF7 roster consisting of eight locomotives. On one particular instance, because other units were being serviced, one CF7 pulled 53 loaded cars and 4 empties over a two-mile stretch of track up a .5% grade at 10 mph. The unit was pulling 850 amps in run 8, but the speed wasn't so bad considering the line is limited to 15 mph restrictions. Usually the railroad has two CF7's pull a 50-car train. In another situation, the railroad used 3 CF7's to pull 248 empty cars.

With shortlines assuming ownership of the CF7's, a proliferation of paint schemes occurred. To name and describe all of the various schemes would be impossible, but the following would be representative of the pride put into the locomotives. The Washington Central had the Seahawk emblem painted on their cabs to honor the totems that are found in that part of the country. Rescar painted their units in a tan paint scheme with red and white trim. Zacky Farms has a bright long hood with a red cab. Cadillac & Lake City painted one unit in a blue scheme, with the outline of Pike's Peak in white on the long hood. Waccamaw Coast Line, now Clinton Terminal, painted their unit in the purple Atlantic Coast Line scheme, complete with ACL-style lettering. Econo-rail had used a solid blue utilitarian design, but has now switched to a solid yellow scheme.

Many CF7's ended up in shortline corporate colors, such as the units that operate on the Pinsly Railroad Family lines; the Pioneer Valley, Florida Midland, Florida Northern and Florida Central are examples. Other corporate schemes represented are the Georgia-Pacific owned lines of Ashley, Drew & Northern and Gloster & Southern, which paints their units in solid green with white stripes on the nose and end of the long hood. The brightest corporate scheme probably has to go to the Genesee & Wyoming, which is orange, yellow and black. This paint scheme is found on the CF7's operating on the Louisiana & Delta and the GWI Switching Services.

Many lines simply adapted the Santa Fe yellow and blue scheme; they may have changed colors, but retained the pattern. And lastly, you have several railroads which simply kept the Santa Fe scheme, added their reporting marks, or in some cases, operated the units completely in Santa Fe paint. One shortline operated a CF7 in the Santa Fe scheme and was involved in a road crossing accident. Since the locomotive was still in Santa Fe paint, that railroad soon found itself facing possible litigation. Because of this accident, the Washington Central CF7's left Barstow, California, with the Santa Fe painted out by Santa Fe workers.

ABOVE: When the Nashville & Eastern sold their CF7's, Commonwealth Railway purchased #2517 and renumbered it to #517. Unit wears the red and grey corporate colors of Rail Link. Photographed late Spring 1991 by Cary F. Poole.

BELOW: Wearing a restenciled warbonnet, Tennken 2518 was seen at Dyersburg, Tennessee, on March 13, 1989. Tennken purchased several CF7's for use on Nashville & Eastern, a related company. Photo by Jimmy W. Barlow.

Compare the paint schemes adorning these two Nashville and Eastern CF7's. The 2525 sports a forest green body with a bright yellow nose, along with yellow lettering and trim. Red safety stripes decorate the frames and the pilot. The "football" on the nose exhibits bold "N&E" initials. The 2523 wears a much more subdued shade of green, with gold lettering and trim. Traditional lettering on the nose replaces the football. The N&E is now completely CF7-free, despite operating a large fleet in the 1980's. The 2525 was photographed at Lebanon, Tennessee, in October 1989, by Kent S. Roberts. The photo of 2523 was taken in Nashville, Tennessee, in late Summer 1989, by Tom Sink.

RIGHT: Texas Industries Cement (TXI) CF7 is the relatively-untouched 2428, at its Hunter, Texas, facility. Note that the unit has spark arrestors on its four stacks and "blatt" horns. The extra side window is very apparent in this view. This unit retains a total Santa Fe paint scheme, with the exception of the small "txi" logo on the cab. Late Winter of 1995, Kel Aiken.

BELOW: Another TXI CF7 is tucked away at its Midlothian, Texas, facility. Except for the small "txi" herald on the cab, this unit is unlettered. The only number is the faint "2447" in the number boards left over from the Santa Fe. The unit still retains its old "blatt" horns. Photographed on November 17, 1992, by Kel Aiken.

LEFT: Midwest Coal Handling has bought 2492 from the Santa Fe for parts. Unit received this attractive coat of primer and was stripped as needed to keep MCH's fleet of CF7's on the move. Unit appears to be intact on the outside, except for part of pilot, a windshield and light lenses. One could only guess as to what is missing from inside. Photo by Cary F. Poole.

Cadillac & Lake City Memories

Now as to my memories of CF7's on the Cadillac & Lake City. First I ought to explain the C&LK started in Michigan about 1964, running between Cadillac and Lake City on an ex-Pennsy branch. They did rather well as a tourist line and hauling Christmas trees out to the Penn Central, until Conrail abandoned the connection about 1980. The company ran the Rock Island line between Goodland, Kansas, and Limon, Colorado, from 1981 to 1984. When they came out here, they held on to the Cadillac & Lake City name, much to the confusion of many people. (We have a Lake City in Colorado, but no one had heard of Cadillac). After they lost the Kansas line to Kyle Railway, they tried to make a go of the Rock Island line from Limon to Colorado Springs. They had only 3-4 employees here. They ran a fan trip in 1985 and were very successful with regular scheduled trains to the 1985 El Paso County Fair in 1985, running 4-5 round trips a day from Falcon (near Colorado Springs), 20 miles to Calhan. Then they started short trips for school children. At this point they enlisted members of the local NRHS chapter as volunteer Trainmen to help in the cars. Several of us, being retired, got real interested and trained as Brakemen and freight Conductors. Then 2 or 3, including myself, trained as Enginemen. I was "set-up" as a qualified Engineman in November, 1987. I logged over 6,000 miles in the next 26 months, over a 60-mile line. Mostly I ran the two CF7's, but I also ran an ex-Alaska Railroad F9 we had for a while, and made 2-3 trips on a UP U23B.

The Cadillac & Lake City got their CF7's in February, 1986, in good clean Santa Fe paint. They tried to paint out the hood name with spray cans that summer, but it was a lost cause. Sometime between December 1986 and February 1987, they decided to renumber the units . The 2489 became #48, and the 2509 became #50 (they just painted out the first and last digit). In September, 1988, a group of volunteers got the proper equipment and did a beautiful job on the 48. I don't remember the exact colors: the blue was darker than the Santa Fe blue. I think the colors were what was available locally, not necessarily railroad colors. I know they first wanted to use maroon or red with yellow in honor of the Rock Island who built the line, but then they found that maroon cost twice as much as blue.

I can't comment on maintenance of the CF7's. Before a run I would inspect the units, using a check list. We would check fluid levels and add water or oil occasionally. Starting the engine was a 10-minute job -- opening cylinder petcocks, turn over the engine to avoid hydro-static lock, close the petcocks, turn on pumps, crank the engine, then finish the check list while the engine warmed up. Nothing difficult; two of us could run through it all and be ready to roll in 15 minutes. Shutting down after a run was quicker -- mostly a lot of switches to turn off.

I did help filling the sand boxes a couple of times. This was tough: man-handling 100 pound bags up on the nose, to the cab roof, then carry them to the rear of the hood.

I think most of us liked the units very much. As a Brakeman I though they were good. The railings and grab irons were well planned: there was a handle wherever you needed it. The steps were slanted out so they were easy to climb and you could stand comfortable on the bottom step while switching. The steps on the U23B were nearly vertical, it was like climbing a book case! Made on trip with a GP9; it wasn't much better. An of course, it was Hell switching with the F9.

The Engineman's visibility was excellent. Our units had the long one piece windshield on the control side. You could almost see the front coupler, so you a good view of the man on the ground when coupling. I occasionally had to make a coupling alone; you could move up until you lost sight of the couplers, then nudge it forward about a foot and make a smooth "joint".

On the road, forward visibility was excellent for both crew members. Running backwards it was good as any hood unit. I often cussed some poor railfan who moaned about the Santa Fe "spoiling a beautiful F-unit." We had no wye at the west end, so the units always faced west. I told then I had no desire to run an F7 backwards 60 miles, with my head twisted around and hanging out the window in the dust, rain or snow. And the Conductor didn't want to stand in the back door with a radio to watch crossings either!

On the negative side, the bell was under the right front step. It regularly got plugged with weeds or snow, requiring squirming around underneath to clean it. Also the windshield wipers were lousy. The air mechanism was noisy and seemed to have only two speeds, either an occasional useless flop back and forth, or madly trying to beat the window frames to pieces with a loud clattering. We didn't use them very often because they didn't wipe well anyway. Whether we needed new blades or to adjust the linkage I can's say.

W never used the toilet. I think it was inoperative, but it was cramped down there, and it was easier to make an unscheduled coffee stop anyway.

The cab heaters were usually drained. They did a good job when they were in service. The air conditioners worked very well.

The two units were different to run. The 50 had a bad vibration in Run 3, which rattled everything in the cab. Your lunchbox would walk around the floor and small articles (including your cup of coffee) would fall off the control stand. I recall the 48 rode smoother. If you pushed the speed limit on the best track up to 35-40 MPH it seemed to settle down and ride very well.

The 48 had a added feature I liked. One of the employees installed a "Transition Forestalling" switch on the control stand, which allowed the Engineman to delay automatic transition when starting. Running a passenger train east out of Falcon (our normal terminal) you ran a fair grade (maybe 0.7%) for about half a mile, then hit a spot where the grade leveled off for a bit before resuming the climb. If you accelerated normally out of the station, the train would be doing 18-20 MPH at the level spot. This is were transition would normally occur, causing slack action which disturbed passengers. Turning on the switch would prevent transition. You would continue to accelerate until the train was stretched out on the grade, doing 25-30 MPH. With the switch off, transition would occur smoothly.

The railroad was limited to about 35 MPH, and had grades up to 1.0%. We had short trains and I don't recall any problem getting enough power.

We used the 48 until the railroad went under in January, 1990. It was taken to Limon to be shipped out.

Gordon C. Bassett

ABOVE: Cadillac & Lake City #50 at Falcon, Colorado on October 17, 1988. This engine was painted by a film company for use in a TV cigarette commercial for use out of the US. The engine was still in Santa Fe paint, so they repainted the blue to get rid of the SANTA FE on the hood, then painted the yellow warbonnet bright red. The commercial used the #50 with 25 assorted boxcars and an ex-Santa Fe caboose. Filming took place in an isolated area between Peyton and Calhan, Colorado. When the filming was completed, the C&LC had a special run to return the boxcars to interchange at Limon, Colorado, on October 23, 1988. This was "The Great Freight of '88". The train included both CF7's 25 boxcars, 2 or 3 C&LC passenger cars and both cabooses. Employees, volunteers and families enjoyed a day-long trip with photo run-by's and a picnic.

BELOW: The "Great Freight of '88", the longest train ever run on the C&LC, with engines 48 and 50, eastbound about 3 miles west of Limon, Colorado. Photo run-by at US 24 overpass. Both photos this page by Gordon C. Bassett.

Miscellaneous CF7 Notes

Amtrak officials reported that the Santa Fe was great to work with; when you called the CMO, the CMO picked-up and handled your questions and problems himself. The "Great Trade" occurred almost by accident. An Amtrak official called ATSF to see what was new, and found out the CF7's were to be sold. Amtrak was in bad need of switchers at the time, and the officer mentioned that Amtrak had the 18 remaining SDP40F's in mothballs in Florida. The Kansas City Southern had looked at them and offered a cash bid of $35,000 each, which Amtrak rejected. Santa Fe offered a package of switchers which included 25 CF7's and 18 SSB1200's in exchange for the big SDP's. It was a match made in heaven; Amtrak got the switchers they needed and Santa Fe got the big road power they wanted -- and each railroad was able to unload locomotive types that didn't fit their operating scheme. When Santa Fe took possession of the SDP40F's, they were regeared to freight service and the D-77 traction motors and wheel assemblies were returned to Amtrak, who badly needed them to replace the earlier types which were taken from E's, F's and older switchers.

When Amtrak took possession of the CF7's they made immediate modifications.

The first thing to go was their air conditioners. This was to reduce maintenance costs and lower the clearance of the units. CF7's placed in Corridor service had their rooftops cleared to reduce the height. This included removal of the air conditioner, the ground plate and even the horns from the roof. The 585 (assigned to Chicago) received the work necessary to install HEP by employee Ed Shipper, but a generator was never put in, but was wired as a pass-through. There was once a plan to convert some Boston-based CF7's to HEP for use as a rescue train out of Albany, but the plan never materialized; a pair of Geeps were used instead. Also, the CF7's assigned to Wilmington and Boston had cab signals installed and speed controls added. Units used in Washington and Philadelphia were assigned to Wilmington, those used in Albany and New Haven were assigned to Boston. When New Haven was closed, heavy repairs for Boston-based units were done in Albany.

When the first batch of CF7's were delivered to Amtrak, many of the steps were bent in transit. Some "detective work" revealed that the steps were smashing against the passenger platform at South Bend, Indiana! For the delivery of the last 20 units or so, the pilots had to be trimmed before shipping. This problem

also occurred to some units being delivered to the Blue Mountain & Reading and had to be straightened out at Conrail's Conway Shops at Pittsburgh, Pennsylvania.

"I'm afraid that I don't have a similar slide of #2594 as you requested. As of Monday, August 12th, I can't get a good one either, since on that date a garbage truck tried to beat our train through a crossing near Bennettsville, SC. It lost, but in the process derailed #2594 and a second engine. #2594 was in the lead and went down for the count." -- Edward A. Lewis, president, Aberdeen and Rockfish Railway

First New York, Susquehanna & Western doublestack train, Sunday August 4, 1985, consist: NYS&W 3004-3000-3002-260-2425-3008 (C430/C430/C430/C420Hi-hood/Leased CF7/C430) Binghamton, New York, to Little Ferry, New Jersey. (Railpace)

Columbus & Greenville bought the MidSouth 7004 for parts, but actually fired it up and ran it (as the 7004) before it quit again-- this time for good. (Courtesy Columbus & Greenville)

WATCO's 106 (former Meridian & Bigbee 106) reportedly will be used to

serve a new WATCO operation in Indianapolis, Indiana, in late April. The WATX 6 & 7 are in Wallula, Washington. WATX 1002 is in Oregon, the Osage 1000 is at a steel mill in Missouri. The ISCX 111 is back to Baytown after serving at Geon Co., and former WATX 5 is now Inman ISCX 5 and sporting a fresh coat of paint. (Courtesy, WATCO)

Econo-Rail may be getting a new paint scheme; watch for E-R CF7's in their new green and white paint. (Courtesy, Econo-Rail)

Mississippi & Skuna Valley is quite pleased with the performance of their CF7, identified as D-5. It has given them reliable service for many years, and will be soon getting new wheels -- they were turned once before. Jeff Sullivan, of M&SV, says on their 21 mile run from Bruce, Mississippi, to Bruce Jct., their con-

nection with the Illinois Central, they can just about coast; they do more braking than throttling! *Photo by Jim Shaw.*

NRE reports that 2632 (former Quad Cities Rocket Dinner Train locomotive) is now leased to Quantum Chemical Co. in Clinton, Iowa. Former Amtrak 593 and 598, along with former MidSouth CF7's 7010, 7012 and 7015 are at Silvis, Illinois. Ex-Amtrak 599 is at Dixmoor, Illinois. (Courtesy of NRE)

Amtrak 578 reportedly was to be used for power on the Nobles Rock Railroad in Minnesota, but it appears that 578 never quite made it. An inspection revealed that the frame was damaged and unsuitable for service, so the prime mover was removed from the 578 by Independent Locomotive Services in Bethel, Minnesota, and transplanted into Rail Equipment & Transportation's RETX 302, a GP9.

Minnesota Commercial 484 is a result of a 1-1/2 year rebuild of former Santa Fe 2484, purchased from NRE at Dixmoor, Illinois. It is named "City of Bayport" *(Photo courtesy Minnesota Commercial Railroad)*

Rail Link sold Carolina & North Western Ry. and now owns Talleyrand Terminal Railroad, the Carolina Coastal Railway and Commonwealth Railway, along with contract switching services. They have been purchased by Genesee & Wyoming, who now operates the largest fleet of CF7's in the world. Rail Link locomotives reportedly to get G&W orange and yellow paint in the future. (Courtesy Rail Link)

Check out the modified spark arrestors on the Fort Worth & Western's Tarantula unit #2473 on the turntable below! *Photograph by Kel Aiken.*

ABOVE: Harvester Grain number 2491 (or #1) operated in this very attractive green and yellow scheme. Notice the drawing of the man with the scythe on the nose of the unit. Photographed at Pampa, Texas, on October 2, 1989, by Walter R. Evans, collection of K.M. Ardinger.

RIGHT: A close-up view of "Cahoots" the Tarantula mascot of the Ft. Worth & Western, as seen on the nose of FWWR 2473 on September 24, 1993. Photo by Wes Carr.

ABOVE: Pee Dee River 2486 is shown at Aberdeen, North Carolina, before lettering and numbers were applied. Photographed early Spring 1989, by Ed Lewis.

BELOW: In between paint schemes and owners, former Maryland and Pennsylvania #1500 (previously lettered for Emons, the holding company for MPA and YKR) is about to become Yorkrail 1500, their Operation Lifesaver unit. It also will receive a herald on the nose celebrating Emons' 25th anniversary. The unit ran in this undecorated fashion for only a short period of time. This is the last CF7 built, leaving Cleburne on March 15, 1978, as Santa Fe 2417. The "blatt" and the chimes are both functional, and give an unforgettable sound when used together! Photograph taken Summer 1996 by Jaime F.M. Serensits.

Index

LEFT: Overhead view of MidSouth Rail #7003 west of Forrest, Mississippi. Photo taken Winter 1987, by Tom Sink.

OPPOSITE PAGE: First train on Gloster Southern Railway, August 5, 1986, at Ethyl, Louisiana. Enroute from Slaughter, Louisiana, to Gloster, Mississippi. Phillip H. Schueth, VP-Operations observes. Photo taken by Louis R. Saillard.

ABOVE: Newton Asphalt has painted their CF7 in a Southern Railway-inspired scheme -- forest green with a white band edged in gold. Unit still carries original "blatt" horn from Santa Fe days, and is former ATSF 2432. As of April 7, 1997, unit remains unnumbered. Photo courtesy of Fred Strother, Plant Superintendent, Newton Asphalt.

BELOW: Redmont Railway 101 has also been Chattooga and Chickamauga 101 and Columbus and Greenville 809, all under the CAGY flag. The CAGY influence shows with the beacon in a protective cage, mounted on the ground plane. Also note that this a two-stacker. Unit was originally Santa Fe 2644, the sixth CF7 produced by the Cleburne shop forces. Photo taken in Red Bay, Alabama, by Tom Sink.

ABOVE: Maryland and Pennsylvania 1504 is about to cross Old Hanover Road, between Hanover and Menges Mills, Pennsylvania in 1996. The 1504 ran light from York that day, and switched the small yard in Hanover, returning with two boxcars. It is former Santa Fe 2425, and sports ditch lights, four stacks, multi-chime horns and a low profile antenna on its ground plate. It also displays the model designation under the cab window. Photo by Jaime F.M. Serensits.

BELOW: Ashley, Drew & Northern 1513 is former Santa Fe 2490. When AD&N bought this unit, Santa Fe painted it at Cleburne before delivery, and AD&N applied the lettering, numbering and nose herald once it was on the property. The AD&N had a reputation for keeping its power immaculate, and this photo is case in point. The 1513 is now assigned to Arkansas, Louisiana and Mississippi, another line owned by Georgia-Pacific. Photo taken Fall 1988 by Tom Sink.

RIGHT: Delta Southern #103 at Sterlington, Lousiana, on January 13, 1993. Notice lack of rooftop air conditioners. Stripes on nose are similar to those of Louisiana & Delta's Allegheny & Eastern CF7's. Photo taken by Louis R. Saillard.

RIGHT: Newton Asphalt's CF7 is reminiscent of the paint scheme adorning Southern Railway diesels. Unit is used to switch facility in Alexandria, Virginia. Photo courtesy of Fred Strother, Plant Superintendent, Newton Asphalt.

ONE FINAL LOOK BACK

ABOVE: The weed spraying train has arrived in Emporia, Kansas, behind two different types of Cleburne rebuilds -- CF7 #2627 and rebuilt GP7 #2216. Photo taken Spring 1982, by C. H. Humphreys, collection of Steve Hottle.

BELOW: Santa Fe 2488 soaks up the sun in Bakersfield, California, on April 25, 1976. Check out that set of horns on the cab roof! Also take note of the other gems in the facility -- GP30's and an Alco switcher, along with those carts to the right of 2488's cab. The 2488 later went back to Cleburne for a square cab and eventually became number 488 on the Keokuk Junction Railway. Photo by Jay Reed.

LEFT: Santa Fe #2649 at Cleburne March 1, 1970, shortly before her official debut as the first CF7. The 2649 had been F7 #262C before rebuilding. Notice the dynamic brakes and the open sideframe. The frames were built from I-beams left over from the manufacture of tri-level autoracks. C. H. Humphreys photo, collection of Steve Hottle.

RIGHT: Looking worse for wear, the 2649, is shown inside the former Reading locomotive shops, awaiting the cutting torch. Notice the absence of number boards and class lights on the rear of the locomotive. Compare with the photo on page 45. Photo by Josh Musser.

LEFT: Irony of ironies, Anthracite Railway Historical Society's CNJ #56D was rebuilt using parts taken from CF7 2649. With the sacrifice of the first CF7 ever built, the cycle had come full circle when the 56D emerged from the shops. Photographed on a fantrip at Nesquehoning, Pennsylvania, by Josh Musser.

Bibliography

Interviews

Mr. Eldon Whitworth, CF7 Program Coordinator
    August 7, 1996
    February 3, 1997

Mr. Jack Carlton-Engineer
    Cleburne Shop Reunion-December 7, 1996

Mr. S. D. Rawlins-Shop personnel
    Cleburne Shop Reunion-December 7, 1996

Mr. James Parker-Engineer
    Cleburne Shop Reunion-December 7, 1996

Mr. W. F. Stepp-Shop personnel
    Cleburne Shop Reunion-December 7, 1996

Books

Berkman, Pamela, History of the ATSF, Bonanza Brompton Book Corp., Greenwich, CT, 1988.

Boyd, Jim, Illinois Central: Monday Morning Rails, Andover Junction, Andover, NJ, 1994.

Carlton, W. E. "Jack", It Took Their Kind, Texian Press, Waco, TX.

Carroll, John, Galveston and the Gulf, Colorado & Santa Fe Railroad, Center for Transportation and Commerce, Galveston, TX, 1985.

EuDaly, Kevin, Santa Fe 1992 Annual, Hyrail Productions, Denver, CO, 1992.

Lewis, Edward A., American Shortline Railway Guide, Kalmbach Books, Waukesha, WI, 1997.

Kerr, James W., 1995-1996 Locomotive Rosters & News, DPA-LTA Enterprises, Inc., Montreal, Canada, 1995.

McCall, John B., Santa Fe's Early Diesel Daze, 1935-1953, Kachina Press, Dallas, TX 1980.

McDonald, Charles W., Diesel Locomotive Rosters, Kalmbach Books, Waukesha, WI, 1992.

McMillan, Joe, Route of the Warbonnets, McMillan Publications, Woodridge, IL, 1981.

McMillan, Joe, Santa Fe Motive Power, McMillan Publications, 1985.

Pinkepank, Jerry A. , The Second Diesel Spotters Guide, Kalmbach Books, Waukesha, WI, 1991.

Pinkepank, Jerry A. and Marre, Louis A., The Contemporary Diesel Spotters Guide, Kalmbach Books, Waukesha, WI, 1991.

Reck, Frank, On Time: History of the Electro-Motive Division of GMC, EMD of GM, 1948.

Reed, Jay, Comprehensive Guide to Industrial Locomotives, Rio Hondo, Santa Rosa, CA, 1995.

Reich, Sy, Diesel Locomotive Rosters, Wayner Publications, New York, NY, June 1973.

Spurrell, Fred, From Streamliners to Bullheads to Hooters, Yakima, WA, 1988

Magazines

Bontrager, David, "GT&I CF7", Mainline Modeler, April 1992, pp. 51-54.

Cardall, Gordon, "The CF7 in HO Scale, Part II," Railmodel Journal, October 1990, pp. 6-7.

Chandler, Craig, "Kitbashed Santa Fe CF7," Railroad Model Craftsman, November 1985, pp. 81-82.

Edmonston, Jim, "Trackside in the Diesel Age: Cleburne Loco Shop," Railroad, February 1978, p. 55.

Chatfield, Scott, "Ugly Duckling of Dieseldom: The EMD/ATSF CF7,"Railmodel Journal, August 1990, pp.42-46.

Flick, Michael, "Product Review - Hallmark CF7", Santa Fe Modeler, March/April 1981, p. 17, 23.

Houston, Mayne Neaves, "Gulf Lines Shop Facilities Are the Pride of Cleburne," Santa Fe Magazine, October 1915, pp. 21-15.

Ingles, J. David, "Ugly Ducklings Disperse," Trains, November 1987.

Lustig, David, "Creatures from Cleburne," Railfan & Railroad, May 1985, pp 44-50.

Middleton, Keel, "Santa Fe Locomotive Rosters," Santa Fe Modeler, July/August 1986, pp. 20-21.

Neubauer, Eric, "The CF7," Railroad Model Craftsman, November 1985, pp. 83-86.

Poole, Cary F., "The Evolution of the CF7: Mainline to Shortline Service," The Railroad Press, Jan/Feb/Mar 1997, pp. 11-21.

Queen, Clyde, Jr., "Paint Shop: Warbonnet CF7," Model Railroader, November 1994, pp. 160-162.

Saillard, Louis R., "Rebirth of the Vicksburg Route: MidSouth Rail: Threefold Growth," Trains, April, 1989, pp. 30-41.

Stephenson, Dick, "National Railway Equipment Company," Pacific Rail News, December 1987.

Thayer, Marshall, "Cleburne Cross-Kit," Railroad Model Craftsman, March 1971, pp. 36-39.

Ziegenhorn, Roger, "Cabs To Hoods - The CF7," Santa Fe Modeler, September/October 1979, pp. 8-10.

Zwernemann, Jim "CF7: A Closer Look at a Crossbreed," Pacific News Magazine, March 1973.

Diesel Era, various issues.

Extra 2200 South, various issues.

Railpace Newsmagazine, various issues.

Santa Fe Modelers Association Newsletter July 1970, #8, p. 2; Aug/Sept. 1970, pp. 12-13; October 1970, p. 9; November 1970, p. 4; December 1970, p. 6; January/February 1971, pp. 11-12.

The Setout, Southeast Texas Chapter NRHS Newsletter, Summer 1996, p5.

The Short Line, vaious issues.

BELOW: Dodge City, Ford & Bucklin #1001, ex-South East Kansas 1001, is seen with a passenger train at Dodge City, Kansas, on July 31, 1990. Photo by Evan Werkema.

BN at Cleburne

As I was leaving Cleburne during the afternoon of December 7, 1996, I noticed the signal turned green permitting a southbound to proceed through town and pass along side of the Cleburne Shops. It was somewhat prophetic to see what appeared; a Burlington Northern coal train lead by some of the newest locomotive technology, three SD70MAC's on the front end, as they passed in front of the Cleburne Machine and Boiler Shops. The BN locomotives reflect the recent merger between BN and the Santa Fe and accounts for why "foreign" power was rumbling along side the Cleburne Shops. One could only speculate that if given the chance, the men and women of the Cleburne Shops could tackle even the newest of locomotive technologies.

ABOVE: Southbound BNSF train rolls by Cleburne's famous smokestack on December 7, 1996. Photo by Cary F. Poole.

REAR COVER TOP: The crews of the Louisiana & Delta and Supreme Sugar pose on their respective locomotives on one of the last runs on L&D's Supreme Branch. The photo shows the train, along with Supreme Sugar Company's 35-ton Plymouth switcher. On the CF7 are Mike Hymel and Willard Neal of L&D, and on the Plymouth is Robert Anderson, of Supreme Sugar. The sugar refinery at Supreme would close in just a couple of weeks, taking away the last customer on the branch. The 303 is sporting new ditch lights, but no classification lights, and has not been relettered since leaving Pennsylvania for Louisiana. Notice how the "3" was stenciled-in over the "1" when it was renumbered it from 103 to 303. Photo taken on September 29, 1995, at Supreme, Louisiana.

CENTER: Columbus and Greenville 808, the first CAGY CF7 to be painted green and gold, is checked over by personnel at the facility in Columbus, Mississippi, on December 27, 1994. Note the placement of a firecracker antenna and warning beacon on ground plane. It appears that a metal cage was fabricated to keep the beacon from being smashed. Also note the old "Delta Route" logo on turntable.

BOTTOM: Crew of Mississippi & Skuna Valley D-5 (Jack Brandon, engineer; Billy Crutchfield, brakeman; Wayne Jones, conductor) pose at Gum's Crossing, 3 miles east of Coffeeville, Mississippi, on October 14, 1987. Note unique placement of bell; it is doubtful that they will ever have problems with tall grass clogging the clapper. All photos on the back cover by Louis R. Saillard.